SOUTHERN ELECTRIC MULTIPLE-UNITS

1898~1948

1
4SUB now BR Class 405 No 4618 meanders towards New
Malden from Raynes Park on the 17.04 Waterloo-
Shepperton service on 18 May 1980.   *Colin J. Marsden*

SOUTHERN ELECTRIC MULTIPLE~UNITS

1898~1948

COLIN J. MARSDEN

LONDON

IAN ALLAN LTD

First published 1983

ISBN 0 7110 1253 9

Published by Ian Allan Ltd, Shepperton, Surrey;
and printed by Ian Allan Printing Ltd at their works
at Coombelands in Runnymede, England

Contents

6PUL No 3007 painted in standard SR green livery with chocolate and cream Pullman car forming the third vehicle, passes under an impressive brick arch bridge near Merstham with a Worthing bound train during the early 1950s.
British Railways

Introduction

Perhaps the least followed of the railway traction types is the electric multiple-unit (emu) train. The majority of the tens of thousands of people from the Southern commuter areas who travel by emu every day to the capital do not, and have not, over the years, given a second look at their rail transport. This volume has been drawn together to cover trains conforming to the basic emu requirement, that were in traffic or being tentatively designed for use on the Southern Railway and its former companies until railway nationalisation at the beginning of 1948.

Vehicles gradually progressed in design, construction methods and passenger comfort from the very sparse, badly lit, unheated and wooden seated original Waterloo & City Railway stock of 1898, to the comparatively luxurious interiors of main line stock of BEL and PUL types which were constructed mainly of steel panels during the 1930s.

During the early 1900s it became apparent to the railway companies of Southern England that to achieve a fast, reliable, frequent and clean passenger service from the inner and outer suburbs which was the future requirement, steam propulsion was not the answer, and during 1903 the LB&SCR obtained Parliamentary powers to electrify its network, using a German overhead power collection system at 6,700V. Development of this continued throughout the early 1900s and through the war years until the late 1920s when the system was finally abandoned and rebuilt to ground third rail operation.

The first of the conventional third rail pick up units emerged during late 1913 on the LSWR, following the Company's decision to electrify its suburban system.

Following the general success of the electric train, electric railway systems by all three of the constituent Southern companies were developing rapidly in the mid-1920s, and from then on electric traction in the south of England has never looked back.

Passenger accommodation on the 1898 built Waterloo & City Railway stock was all one class — third, but on the LB&SCR 6,700V system first and third class seating was provided. The majority of subsequent dc units were also equipped for dual class accommodation, and the real break in the tradition came in 1944 when Eastleigh Works constructed unit No 4102 to all third class requirements. During the 1940s first class seating on suburban stock was withdrawn, as few passengers were prepared to pay the extra fare for the extra comfort on their comparatively short journeys.

From 1956 third class accommodation was reclassified to second on mainline and suburban units alike.

Although some of the 4SUB units that were still operating during 1982 were well over 30 years old, due to the high standards of workmanship and the nature of the robust equipment used in their construction, these units, with little maintenance would be able to continue in traffic for many years, but due to modern replacement stock being under construction this seems very unlikely.

Over the past 20 years many redundant emu sets have been, after withdrawal, taken into departmental stock as de-icing, mobile classrooms or stores units, giving the emu enthusiast a chance to see these fine sets still in action, but not in passenger service.

Although not strictly pre-1948 units the 4DD and early 4EPB types have been included in this volume, as tentative plans for their introduction were well underway prior to January 1948.

I would like to thank the many people who have assisted with research for this project, particularly Mr J. N. Faulkner and BR (Southern) Public Affairs Office, Waterloo, for assistance with early photographs, Mrs J. Marsden for secretarial work and finally the publishers for giving me freedom with the selection of illustrations and preparation of final manuscripts.

Colin J. Marsden
Surbiton
November 1982

Coach Classifications ~ used within EMU type stock

Note

Third class accommodation was altered to second class with effect from 1956.

First class accommodation was removed from suburban EMU stock from October 1941.

DTC   Driving Trailer Composite
DTCL   Driving Trailer Composite Lavatory
DTLV   Driving Trailer Luggage Van
DTT   Driving Trailer Third

M   Motor
MBC   Motor Brake Composite
MBT   Motor Brake Third
MBSO   Motor Brake Second Open
MBTL   Motor Brake Third Lavatory
MBTO   Motor Brake Third Open
MBTP   Motor Brake Third Pullman
MLV   Motor Luggage Van

T   Trailer
TBSL   Trailer Brake Second Lavatory

TC   Trailer Composite
TCK   Trailer Composite Corridor
TCL   Trailer Composite Lavatory
TCP   Trailer Composite Pullman
TF   Trailer First
TFK   Trailer First Corridor
TFK(P)   Trailer First Corridor (Pantry)
TFP   Trailer First Pantry
TRB   Trailer Restaurant Buffet
TRG   Trailer Restaurant Griddle
TRT   Trailer Restaurant Third
TS   Trailer Second
TSK   Trailer Second Corridor
TSP   Trailer Second Pantry
TT   Trailer Third
TTK   Trailer Third Corridor
TTO   Trailer Third Open

3
The Southern's most famous electric train the 'Brighton Belle'. In this illustration a single five-car set passes Bosham station painted in the final livery of blue and grey on 8 April 1972 with an RCTS Railtour. *John Scrace*

Original Waterloo & City Railway stock

It was during the mid-1890s that work commenced on construction of the London City extension line, later known as the Waterloo & City Railway. Rolling stock for the line was ordered from the firm of Jackson & Sharp of Wilmington, USA, who sent the major components to England for final assembly at the railway workshops at Eastleigh. These American built trains were of four-car formation, a single ended motor car at each end with two trailers in between. Passenger accommodation was poor for the 1 mile 46ch journey, as the seating provided was only wooden, with no heating and hardly any lighting. Five of these four-car trains entered service when the line opened to the public on 8 August 1898. During 1899/1900 Dick Kerr & Co built five single double ended cars for use on the line during slack periods. Further coaches were constructed for the line in 1904 when the Electric

4
A very rare illustration of the original Waterloo & City railway stock, showing a complete four-car train of 1898 Jackson & Sharp stock, parked in the sidings at Waterloo. The lattice gates can clearly be seen between the cars. It is interesting to note the difference between draw gears of the USA built stock and that designed and built by Dick Kerr Ltd. *British Railways*

Tramway Company of Preston built two trailers as spares and the LSWR works at Eastleigh built four further trailers in 1922 to augment the 1898 built four-car sets to five-car formations. Coaches were of an all wood construction and painted in dark brown livery.

After 1922 when five-car trains were in operation, 'sets' were then referred to by the letters A to E, and the last known operating formations of the sets during early 1940 were:

A — 10, 21, 22, 23, 9.
B — 8, 24, 25, 26, 5.
C — 6, 27, 28, 29, 12.
D — 4, 31, 32, 33, 2.
E — 3, 34, 35, 36, 11.
Leaving cars — 1, 7, 30 as spare.
And double ended cars 13-17 as single cars for off peak running.

Power equipment for all trains was provided by Siemens, with each 'power car' developing some 120hp from two directly wound armatures on to both axles of one bogie, traction power being provided by the line's own power house at Waterloo, where five

coal fired boilers supplied steam to drive six Bellis & Morcom engines which were coupled to Siemens bipolar dynamos, developing 200kW. This power supply system stayed in operation for only a short period and was replaced when the LSWR surface local lines were electrified during 1915, from then on power was taken direct from the new surface power house situated just outside the main station. The line operated a superb passenger service with very primitive equipment until late in 1938 when it was decided to refurbish the line with new equipment and more modern rolling stock. The last of the original coaches were removed from the Waterloo & City line during November 1940 after delivery of the new stock, and were taken to Eardley Sidings near Steatham Common and Gatwick where all were cut up between 1941 and 1950.

It is interesting to note that this original electric stock was the first to carry electric head and tail marker lights (two red lights at each end of the train) a system which is still in force today.

Original car numbering

1-12	original 1898 Jackson Sharp single ended motor cars
13-17	Dick-Kerr 1899/1900 double ended motor cars.
21-30	original 1898 Jackson Sharp trailer cars.
31-32	Electric Tramway Co, Preston, 1904 spare trailers.
33-36	LSWR 1922 additional trailer cars.

5
The very sparse but somewhat elegant interior of an 1898 built Jackson & Sharp trailer vehicle. The seating provided was of wood benching only, while leather 'hangers' were provided for standing passengers. It is interesting to note that as well as having advertisements above cant rail height, some are affixed to the windows including a rather pleasant oval shaped Royal Exchange Assurance embellishment on the right hand side of the car. *British Railways*

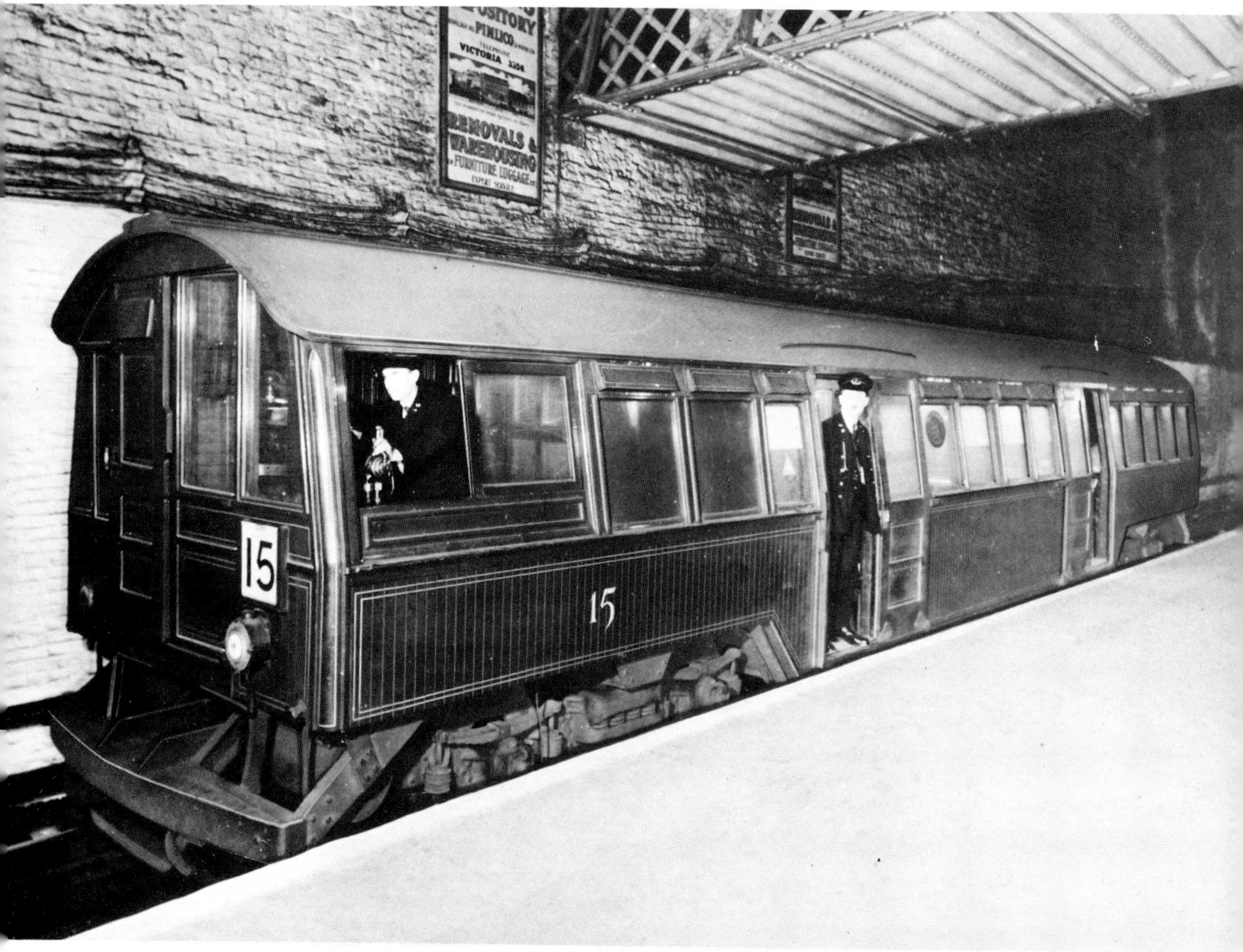

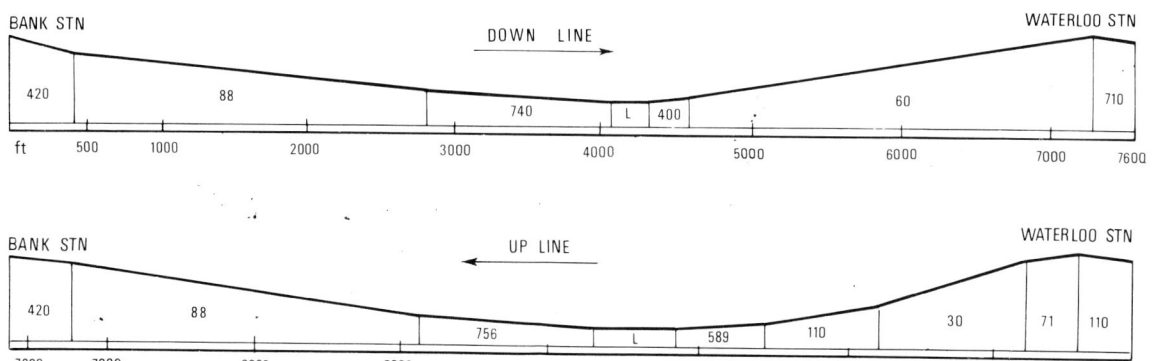

6
Double ended Dick Kerr motor car No 15 stands singly at
Waterloo during 1940 just prior to removal from the line.
The front end emergency door on these Dick Kerr built
vehicles was of the sliding type, as can be seen in this view
taken from the motor end.   *British Railways*

Fig 1: Gradient profile, Waterloo & City Line.

BANK STN   DOWN   LINE →   WATERLOO STN

| 420 | 88 | | 740 | L | 400 | | 60 | 710 |

ft   500   1000   2000   3000   4000   5000   6000   7000   7600

BANK STN   ← UP   LINE   WATERLOO STN

| 420 | 88 | | 756 | L | 589 | 110 | | 30 | 71 | 110 |

7600   7000   6000   5000   4000   3000   2000   1000   ft   0

LB&SCR Overhead stock

It was in 1903 that the LB&SCR obtained powers to electrify its network and it was soon decided to adopt a German design of electric propulsion system where an overhead mounted cable carrying high-tension single-phase alternating current would be erected. The voltage decided upon was 6,700V ac which was to be supplied by the London Electric Supply Corporation from their power house at Deptford, and distributed via the railways sub-power house at Queens Road (Peckham). By late in 1903 the LB&SCR had decided that the first line that they would electrify would be the South London line between London Bridge and Victoria via Denmark Hill and work soon commenced. The original rolling stock was provided by eight three-car trains, built by the Metropolitan Amalgamated Carriage & Wagon Co Ltd, the formation of which was two third class driving motor brakes, with a first class trailer between. The length of each coach was 63ft 7in long by 9ft 3in wide, seating was provided for 74 first and 144 third class passengers. The external appearance of these trains was smart being of a panelled appearance and the livery applied was umber brown on the lower panels and mid-cream on the upper. Power equipment was provided by four 115hp Winter Eichberg traction motors, two under each driving compartment, each supplied with its power via a transformer reducing the 6,700V ac to a more controllable 750V for traction purposes. Power collection was by roof mounted bows, two of which were provided above each driving cab, one for each running direction. Public service commenced on 1 December 1909 with frequent trains which proved to be well accepted by the public and after only a short period of operation was declared a total success, with only the minimum number of failures due to defective equipment being recorded.

Before many years of service had passed, the formations of trains were giving cause for concern. During off peak periods the trains were running with many empty seats but during the 'Rush Hours' too few seats were provided, while far too many first class seats were being provided at all times. From 1910 alterations to these three-car sets were carried out when the first class trailers were removed and placed in traffic as standard locomotive hauled vehicles. A new fleet of driving trailers was converted from bogie suburban sets and were coupled with the remaining

South London driving motor cars, to provide two-car motor sets, equipped for multiple-unit operation of up to three units.

As was the success of the South London line, it was not long before further routes were added to the system. The next line to be equipped was the line from Victoria/London Bridge to Crystal Palace via Streatham Hill, which opened on 12 May 1911 and operated a regular service from 1 June 1911. Overhead power equipment was continued to Norwood Junction/Selhurst where a carriage stabling and servicing shed was built. The section of line between Peckham Rye Junction to Tulse Hill and Leigham Junction/West Norwood was brought into use from March 1912 with a full passenger service starting on 1 June 1912 after new power generating equipment was installed.

Stock for this line was provided in the form of 30 motor coaches and 30 driving trailers built by the same company that provided stock for the SLL during 1908/9, these were augmented by a further 30 driving trailers built at the LB&SCR works at Lancing. Due to loading restrictions at Crystal Palace the total width of stock was only 8ft 0in by 57ft 7½in long. The livery applied to these sets was umber brown. These trains were less attractive than the original SLL stock as they lacked some of the ornate decorations previously carried. Trains normally operated in three-car formations with a motor car in the middle and a driving trailer at each end, trains were not normally operated formed of more than six cars, but it was known for trains to be used formed of up to eight vehicles.

Further extensions of the systems were projected during 1913 for the remainder of the LB&SCR suburban network, but with the outbreak of World War 1 during 1914 these plans were severely restricted, as the power and traction equipment was not now available. After the war ended in 1918 it was agreed by the LB&SCR to electrify their lines to Brighton/Eastbourne and Coulsdon North, but as time proved, only the route to Coulsdon North and Sutton was eventually done. This opened to the public on 1 April 1925, some two years after the amalgamation of the LBSCR/LSWR/SECR to form the Southern Railway in 1923.

Stock for the Coulsdon North/Sutton extensions was provided by 21 motor vans (known as milk vans), 60 driving trailers and 20 trailers. The 'milk vans' were of an unusual design as they were virtually an electric locomotive, with a driving cab being provided at each end, with electrical equipment, guard's van and luggage accommodation between; the length of these vehicles was 42ft 1in and their weight was 62ton, being built by the Metropolitan Carriage, Wagon & Finance Co Ltd of Birmingham. The total power output of these vehicles was 1,000hp. Trains normally operated in five-car formations, viz: driving trailers third class, composite driving trailer, motor van, composite trailer, driving trailer third class, during peak periods up to two sets were operated in multiple. The livery applied to stock was the new Southern Railway green and the old LB&SCR umber brown. After the formation of the Southern Railway the stock became distinguished into three main classifications: SL — South London, CP — Crystal Palace, and CW — Coulsdon and Wallington. Due to the larger part of the Southern Railway already adopting the third rail electrification system the SR Board decided to abandon the overhead system and an announcement was made in August 1926 that all lines would be converted to third rail operation.

The first line to close was the line from London Bridge/Victoria to Streatham Hill and Crystal Palace on 17 June 1928 and the other Crystal Palace services closed from 3 March 1929. As the Crystal Palace stock became spare it gradually took over the duties of the CW sets, which finally ceased operation on 22 September 1929. The majority of vehicles were taken to Peckham Rye shops and converted into dc electric stock, while the milk vans were converted at Eastleigh into goods brakes.

7
One of the original eight three-car sets built during 1909 for the Victoria-London Bridge via Denmark Hill route. The livery carried is umber brown with light cream upper panels. Above the guard's brake/motorman's compartment a large power collection bow can be seen.
Bucknall Collection/Ian Allan Library

8
A three-car train of Crystal Palace line stock stands at Victoria during the early 1920s. These sets designed for the Crystal Palace line contained first class accommodation in the driving cars (three compartments) and housed their power collection equipment above the trailer vehicle. In this view car 4010 stands nearest the camera. *British Railways*

9
Painted in Southern Railway livery a Coulsdon North/Sutton extension power car carrying number 10101 stands in the yard of Metropolitan Carriage Wagon & Finance Company works at Saltley. When in operation these vehicles, known as milk vans were formed in the centre of a five car formation. Driving positions were provided in these power cars but were seldom used. *British Railways*

10
Two two-car SL units approach Clapham station on a Victoria-London Bridge working towards the end of overhead operation on 17 March 1928. The ground third rails for 660V operation were already in situ when this illustration was taken. This photograph clearly shows the different widths of the 1910 converted driving trailer leading in each set and the original wide bodied 1909 built driving motor (trailing in each set). *H. C. Casserley*

L&SWR three-car motor sets

It was early in 1913 that the L&SWR announced its intention to undertake large scale electrification of suburban lines radiating from Waterloo to Wimbledon via East Putney, Waterloo to Kingston (Roundabout), Hampton Court, Shepperton, Hounslow loop lines and both routes to Guildford. Power for these 'new' railways was to be provided by the L&SWR from their own power house which was to be constructed at Durnsford Road (Wimbledon). Work soon commenced and the power-house was ready for operation during late 1913. The stock for these lines was constructed/converted at the L&SWR workshops at Eastleigh, where 84 three-car sets were constructed carrying running numbers E1-E84. Each train was made up of a motor coach, trailer coach, and motor coach; motor coaches were provided with traction equipment mounted on the bogie under the driver's cab with a guards van directly behind. The total power output per unit was 1,100hp provided by four 275hp motors, all electrical and control equipment being supplied by the British Westinghouse Company. Electrical control equipment was carried behind the driver's cab, being ventilated by side louvres, brakes were of the quick acting Westinghouse type, with air being supplied by two compressors one being mounted under each motor car. Power collection was achieved by four slippers one mounted on each side of the power bogies, power was transferred on to a power train line, so that it was available through the train even if only one slipper was in contact with the third 'live' rail. Passenger accommodation was provided for first and third class passengers with a total of 185 passengers being carried in a three-car set. This was increased to 236 during 1934 when vehicles were rebuilt and mounted on longer 62ft steel underframes. Units commenced passenger operation on 25 October 1915 when a service was instigated between Waterloo and Wimbledon via East Putney. Passenger services on the Kingston loop and Shepperton lines commenced during January 1916 followed by the Hounslow loop during March and Hampton Court during June. The new Guildford line was electrified only as far as Claygate and was ready for use from 20 November 1916, further electrification of this route was not undertaken until after the end of World War 1.

All 84 sets were converted from 1904 built four-car steam hauled suburban sets, and mounted on a wooden underframe, coach ends were of the 'Torpedo' style with two windows and a centre headcode between, the headcode box being a vertical rectangle illuminated from behind with an opaque glass panel in front. The train destination — a letter of the alphabet was then fixed as a stencil in front. The letters used during the early years were:

V	Waterloo-New Malden-Richmond-Waterloo
$\bar{S}$	Waterloo-Wimbledon-Shepperton
H	Waterloo-Hampton Court
$\bar{P}$	Waterloo-East Putney-Wimbledon
$\bar{V}$	Waterloo-Richmond-New Malden-Waterloo
$\bar{O}$	Waterloo-Richmond-Hounslow-Waterloo
O	Waterloo-Hounslow-Richmond-Waterloo
I	Waterloo-Claygate
S	Waterloo-Shepperton via Richmond

Units were fitted with standard screw shackle couplings on unit ends, with the control and power jumpers mounted on the body frames. Between unit coaches the connections were by a three link coupling with one centre buffer, as well as air and power/control cables. The livery applied was green with the Company's insignia applied in gold.

Units were allocated to the new servicing shed built at Wimbledon, and were later cared for at the Strawberry Hill emu depot which was a former steam shed, when the steam allocation was transferred to the new Feltham shed from 1921. Trains were normally operated in three-car sets, but during peak periods two sets were often coupled together, giving a running total of six coaches.

The unit numbers E1-E84 were carried until the 1923 grouping when unit numbers 1201-1284 were allocated, motor cars were numbered in the 80xx/94xx series. All units were later augmented into 4SUB formations and renumbered into the 41xx/42xx fleets. After the 1923 grouping, the units were repainted in Southern Railway green and were given standard 'Southern Railway' insignia on their body sides.

11
An early view of an L&SWR three-car motor set displaying running number E73. This illustration, although slightly touched up by a Company artist, clearly shows the distinctive body styling of these sets. As this is a rear three-quarter view the red oil tail lamp will be seen affixed above the buffer on the driver's side. *GEC Traction Ltd*

12
Two L&SWR three-car motor sets with unit No E40 leading depart from the southern end of East Putney tunnel and pass Cromer Road signalbox. The large girder style frames of this stock are apparent in this view. *British Railways*

13
Two three-car South Western motor sets, with unit No 1210 formerly No E10 departs from Hounslow station with a Waterloo (W) — Waterloo (W) roundabout service during the mid-1920s. Note the train duty number affixed inside the fireman's side window.

Trailer sets

In 1920 the passenger flow on the South Western was such that it necessitated the introduction of either a more frequent service, or the present service required strengthening; the latter choice was adopted and 24 two-coach third class only trailer units were introduced. These 48 coaches were converted from standard loco hauled stock at Eastleigh works. During conversion work the coaches were close coupled and fitted with emu type jumpers, as well as quick acting Westinghouse triple valves. Internal layout of coaches was: one coach with eight compartments, and the other with nine. The length of each two-car set varied between 105ft and 107ft; the width was 8ft 10½in and the total weight 46ton. Numbering after the 1923 grouping was 1001-1024. Thirteen further trailer sets Nos 1025-1037 were converted in 1925 for use with newly built 3SUB units Nos 1285-1310, these trailer sets were converted from LBSCR 1921 built trailer thirds, and after conversion they measured 115ft 2in long, seated 180 third class passengers, and weighed 51ton.

1925/6 saw an introduction of trailer sets on the Eastern Section, these were numbered in the 1051-1120 series and were formed of converted LBSCR nine compartment bogie thirds, normally these trailers would run as pairs, but it was not unknown for single car running to be seen, particularly in the early years. Dimensions were the same as the 1025-1037 batch. Following the 1928/9 electrification programme more batches of trailer sets were formed, sets numbered 1121-1167 were a mixture of SECR and LSWR stock, with each two-car set being formed of an ex-SECR eight compartment bogie, being close coupled to an ex-LSWR 11 compartment vehicle. A further batch of sets were converted from similar stock during 1930 and numbered in the 1188-1194 range. Yet another fleet of trailer sets were converted during the late 1920s from ex-LBSCR stock and numbered 1168-1187, of these sets 1168-1180 were converted from overhead CP motor vehicles and 1181-1187 were formed of one ac trailer coach and a former steam hauled coach; this batch measured 115ft 2in in length and weighed 50ton, seating was provided for between 180-185 passengers. Sets numbered 1195-1198 were placed in traffic during 1934 and were converted from ex-LSWR eight compartment vehicles. These sets were longer than all pre-

viously described types measuring 129ft 4in, with a total weight of 54ton. These four sets did not remain in traffic for long, as a mass reorganisation of trailer sets commenced during 1934. Fifty one units were altered and reformed to consist of a nine compartment LBSCR and a 10 compartment LSWR vehicle. Some vehicles by now had been rebuilt with half steel bodies — all units reformed in the 1934 shuffle were renumbered in the 1038-1120 fleet. During this reformation some early vehicles, mainly of LBSCR origin were withdrawn, while others were used during 1937-8 in the formation of more trailer units carrying Nos 989-1000 and 1199-1200. Many of the trailer cars remained in use for several years with the majority becoming the second trailer when 3SUB units were strengthened to 4SUBs during the war years.

14
This trailer set No 1091 formed of ex-LB&SCR cars stands at Hayes during April 1947 with car 9087 nearest the camera. The multiple-unit control block containing power/control and lighting connections can be seen mounted across the end of the car midway up the body. *H. C. Hughes*

15
LBSCR trailer set No 1064 with car 9188 nearest the camera stands coupled to 3SUB unit No 1630 at Hayes during April 1947. The emu jumper cables can be seen connected to the trailer car. The trailer cars were fitted with standard Westinghouse quick acting triple valves, and their heating and lighting power was transferred from the adjacent emu power car. *H. C. Hughes*

16
With set No 1176 displayed on the end, two-coach trailer set formed of former CP type overhead motor vehicles of 1911 build stand at Hayes during November 1946. Power, control and lighting cable connections will be seen on the nearest end. *H. C. Hughes*

3SUB

The first 3SUB (three-car suburban) units to enter traffic did so during 1925 when the Southern Railway introduced a fleet of 55 units, for use on their recently electrified Western and Eastern Sections. Twenty-six units were built for the Western Section mounted on short frames carrying running numbers 1285-1310, construction of the coaches was divided between the Metropolitan Carriage Wagon & Finance Company and the Birmingham Railway Carriage & Wagon Co Ltd. All electrical and control equipment being provided by Metropolitan-Vickers Ltd. Coaches were steel panelled on wooden framing with the front ends resembling the original three-car motor sets (E1-E84). Seating was provided for 48 first and 170 third class passengers. The units built for the Eastern Section were numbered 1496-1524 and were mounted on standard length frames. The construction of these units was carried out by the Metropolitan Carriage Wagon & Finance Company and the Birmingham Railway Carriage & Wagon Company. Generally units were of the same appearance as the Western Section sets, but seating was provided for 56 first and 180 third class passengers. Further sets were introduced on the Eastern Section during 1926 when units numbered 1401-1495 and 1525-1534 entered traffic, being converted at Ashford from SECR steam stock. The internal layout and seating was the same as on the 1496-1524 fleet. Sets numbered 1601-1630 entered traffic during late 1928 and were used on the Central section, these also were converted from former SECR steam stock, and were mainly used on 1928 electrified lines.

Further units for the 1928 electrification programme were numbered 1631-1657, and entered traffic during early 1929 these were converted from LBSCR suburban sets, conversion work being carried out at Ashford and Brighton works, five further sets entered traffic during 1932 of the same basic design and were numbered 1797-1801, the last unit of which was renumbered 1600 during April 1934.

The Western Section converted some of its steam stock during 1928 into three-car sets which were numbered in the 1658-1701 series, during 1930 units 1773-1785 entered traffic, and were of the same design, both series closely following the design of the original third rail electrics of 1913 vintage. Early in 1931 11 sets emerged from the works carrying

numbers 1786-1796, these were converts from LSWR 1901 built six-wheel suburban vehicles. LSBCR vehicles were converted to provide units 1702-1772 for the 1928/30 electrification programme. It is interesting to note that the cars of units 1717-1769 and 1772 were rebuilds from original LBSCR overhead stock, of all three types. Additional three-car suburban units were converted for the Western Section during 1934/37, all were converted from LSWR stock at Eastleigh and numbering was 1585-1594, 1579-1584. Minor detail differences existed between the two types, the 1585 fleet weighed 109ton while the 1579 design weighed a total of 112ton. The majority of these 3SUB units were later augmented into 4SUBs by the addition of a trailer car taken from the original two-car trailer sets or by the addition of all steel trailers constructed at Eastleigh. The last 3SUB units in operation were converted during 1949, the final 3SUB formations operating on the Waterloo-Hounslow loop line where platform lengths were short.

Unit No 1782 remained in departmental traffic as a mobile classroom for CM&EE staff for many years first carrying the number S10 and later O53.

17
Two 1925 built 14xx three suburban sets approach Mitcham Junction on 29 June 1938 with a trailer set marshalled between. Shortly after this illustration was taken the trailer sets were all disbanded. *R. E. Tustin*

18

A superb photograph of two 3SUB sets, with unit No 1618 formed of converted SECR steam stock slowly departing from Tadworth station on the Tattenham Corner branch, past a lower quadrant signal mounted on a concrete post. This posed photograph of an immaculate ex-shops unit was taken during the autumn of 1927. *GEC Traction Ltd*

19

Five three-car sets entered traffic during late 1931/early 1932 to assist with the 1928 electrification programme. Unit numbers allocated were 1797-1801 but during 1934 when the SR required the 18xx number range for their SL stock, the last unit No 1801 was renumbered 1600. Here No 1600 stands at New Beckenham station with a Charing Cross to Hayes train during November 1946. *H. C. Hughes*

20

Another 3SUB set formed of former SECR vehicles arrives at Chelsfield station with a Charing Cross-Sevenoaks stopping service during the mid-1940s. *J. N. Faulkner Collection*

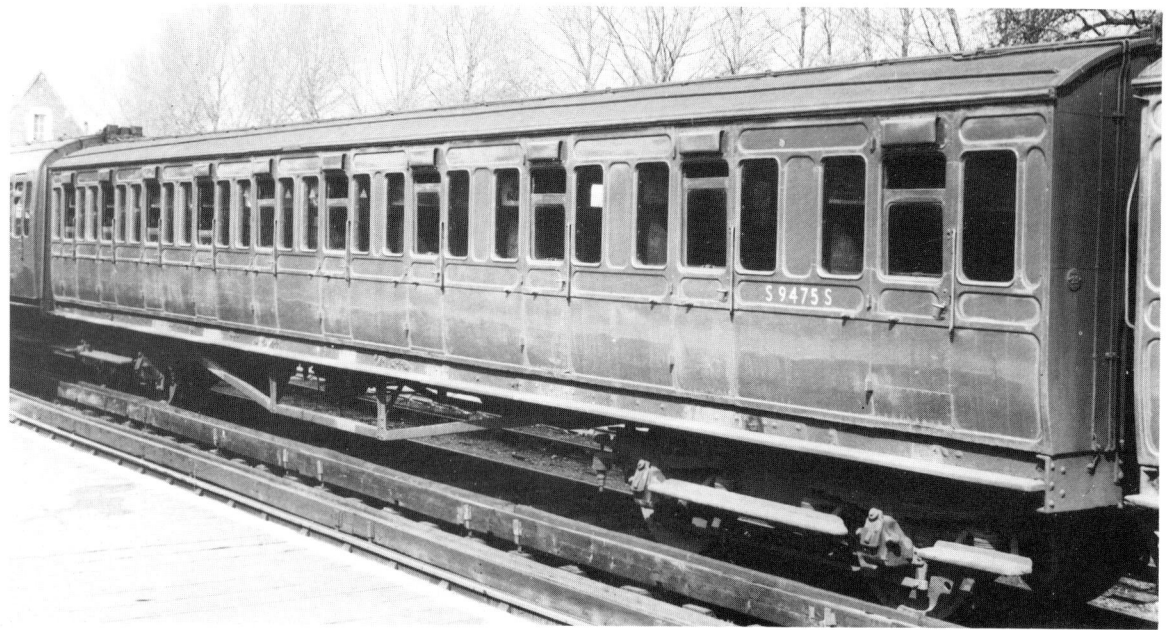

21
Trailer second No S9475S formerly a trailer composite of LBSCR 3SUB unit No 1764 stands formed into a four-car unit at Hampton Court during 1956. This vehicle, like the majority of others in the series 1702-1772, was converted from former ac overhead cars. *G. M. Kichenside*

22
Marshalled between the two Driving Motor Brake Vehicles of 3SUB units was a Trailer Composite providing accommodation for 56 first class passengers in seven compartments, and 15 third class passengers in two compartments at the outer ends of the coach. Here TC No 9600 from unit No 1421 stands separated from the remainder of the unit clearly showing the MCB automatic coupling. *Locomotive Publishing Company*

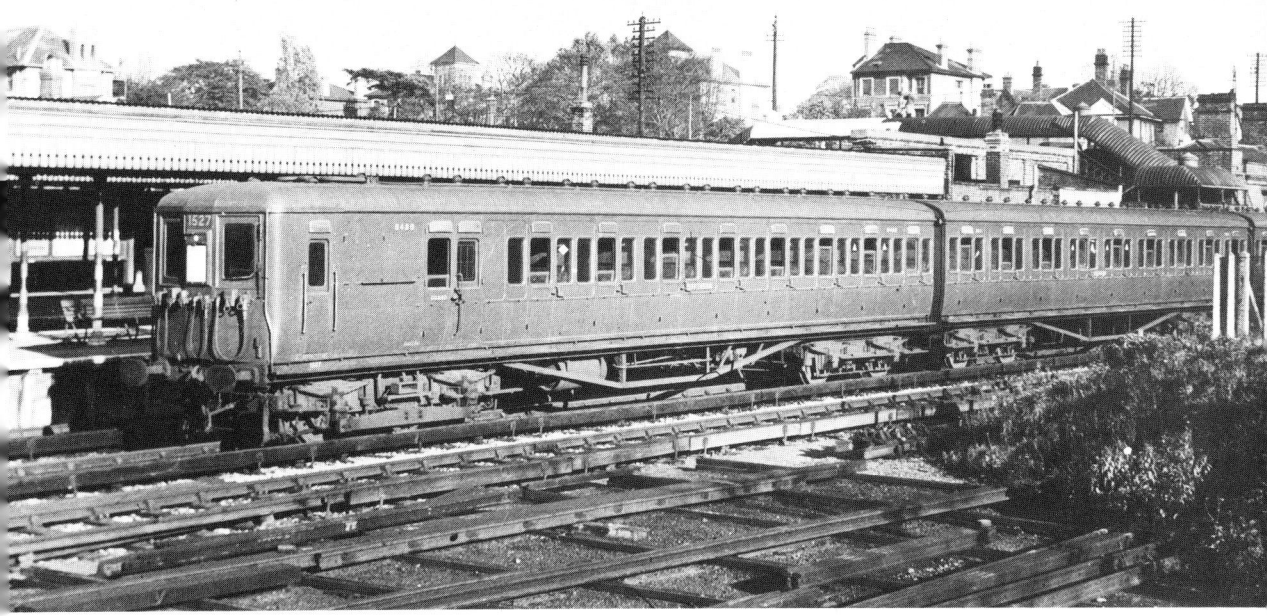

23
Converted to an emu from SECR steam stock in 1926, Eastern Section unit No 1527 stands at Beckenham Junction during November 1946. The sign in the window of the first compartment behind the guard's brake van indicated a Ladies Only compartment, while the triangular signs on the seventh compartment would indicate No Smoking. Note running number painted under driver's door. *H. C. Hughes*

24
The Southern's 3SUB fleet did not escape World War 2 enemy action. The two units illustrated here Nos 1278/1496, stand outside Wimbledon Park on 4 July 1944 after an over-night air raid. Both of these vehicles were subsequently rebuilt after hostilities finished and remained in traffic for many years, both being subsequently converted to four-car units. *British Railways*

25
3SUB No 1303 was converted into a four-car unit during 1947 and renumbered 4318. The new trailer vehicle being of an all steel type constructed at Eastleigh and closely resembling the 41xx 4SUB vehicles then under construction. Unit No 4318 arrives at St Mary Cray on 2 May 1959 bound for Holborn. *R. C. Riley*

2SL and 2WIM

These two different types of unit have been grouped together in this volume, as both were of the same external appearance, and were converted from former overhead ac stock.

2SL units These eight sets were converted at Peckham Rye shops from the original 16 driving vehicles built for the South London Line (SLL) in 1908/9. Each 'new' unit was formed of a driving motor coach and a driving trailer, with all power and control equipment mounted under the motor vehicle. Units commenced operation in their new form from May 1929. The internal layout of the vehicles was: driving motor coach — seven third class compartments, connected by a side gangway, driving trailer — six third and two first class compartments; again the third class compartments were connected by a side gangway. First class seating was in single compartments with side doors, seating was provided for 16 first and 108 third class passengers. Traction equipment was supplied by Metrovic and units had a total of 550hp available. The total length of a two-car set was 127ft 2in while the width was 9ft 6in meaning that these vehicles were not allowed to operate over other routes where the normal operating restriction of 9ft 3in width existed. When converted, the units were numbered 1901-1908, but this was altered to 1801-1808 during early 1934. Carriage numbering for driving motor cars was 8723-8730 and for driving trailers 9751-9758. One unit No 1807 was withdrawn during 1940 after suffering war damage, but the others remained in traffic until the 1950s with the last unit being withdrawn during September 1954. One interesting feature of these units is the lower roof above the driver's cab/guard's compartment; this was the former overhead bow position when in ac service.

2WIM sets This fleet consisted of only four units, which were converted from the eight first class trailer cars built in 1908/9 for the SLL line. After being taken out of SLL use in 1910 and being used for the next 19 years as locomotive hauled first class vehicles on the Brighton main line, all were converted back to electric unit operation at the Peckham Rye shops during 1929. One car of each set was fitted with traction equipment, while the other was converted as a driving trailer vehicle. In the driving motor coaches, seating was provided in seven third class compartments, con-

nected by means of a side corridor, while the driving trailer cars provided accommodation in two first and four third class compartments. Total seating was provided for 16 first and 91 third class passengers, overall dimensions for these units was length: 127ft 4in, and width: 9ft 3in. The unit numbers allocated were 1909-1912 when converted in 1929. This was altered to 1809-1812 during 1934. Driving motor coach numbers were 9818-9821 while the driving trailers carried numbers 9951-9954. All units were withdrawn during 1954. During the 1930s and 1940s it was not uncommon for WIM units to be used on the SLL line or visa versa. Train formations on both lines were normally a single two-coach set, but during peak periods two units were worked in multiple on the South London line. On the Wimbledon-West Croydon line, due to the bay platform at West Croydon only housing two coaches, formations were limited.

26
2SL No 1805 formerly No 1905 slowly departs from Mitcham station on the Wimbledon-West Croydon line with the 12.32 service from Wimbledon on 23 October 1954. Although converted for use on the South London line it was quite regular for these units to operate on the Wimbledon-West Croydon line. *J. J. Smith*

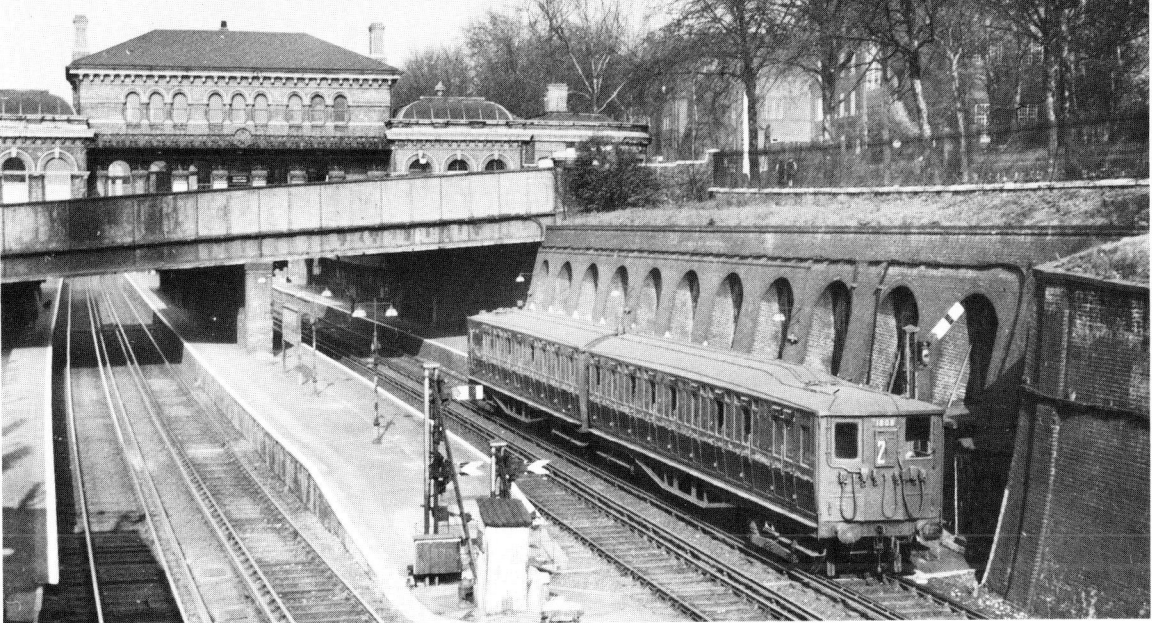

27
Carrying the South London line headcode -2, 2SL set
No 1806 formerly No 1906 arrives at Wandsworth Road
station bound for Victoria during the mid-1940s. The slightly
lower cab roof — a trademark of this type of unit — was
where the ac power pick-up was housed. *H. C. Casserley*

28
Passing under the road bridge and impressive station
buildings at Denmark Hill, 2SL No 1808 formerly No 1908
departs bound for Victoria on a bright 19 April 1953. The
lower cab roofs are clearly visible in this view. *R. C. Riley*

29
2WIM No 1810 formerly 1910 stands in the bay platform at
West Croydon after arriving from Wimbledon on 31 March
1951. Due to restricted clearances on many routes this
9ft 6in wide stock was confined to the intended route.
Late R. Kirkland

4LAV

The first main line electric multiple unit rolling stock constructed was this batch of 33 four-car sets, built at the Eastleigh carriage and wagon works. Construction commenced during 1930 with the first unit emerging during mid-1931, and the last during late 1932. These new main line units were classified as 4LAV (four-car lavatory) and were intended for use on the Victoria-Brighton/Worthing line, operating on semi-fast and slow services. SR numbering given was 1921-1953 which was changed to Nos 2921-2953 during 1937. The formations of units was MBT (Motor Brake Third), TC (Trailer Composite), TCL (Trailer Composite/lavatory) and another MBT. The MBT cars had a full width driver's cab, with guards van behind; passenger accommodation was provided in seven third class compartments. TC coach accommodation was provided in the way of four third and five first class compartments, with a side connecting corridor. During the later years three of the first class compartments were down-graded. Seating in the TCL car was reduced by the positioning of two toilets (one at each end) and passenger accommodation was in five first and three third class compartments. Total seating for a complete four-car unit was 70 first, and 204 third, while overall length of a set was 257ft 2½in, with a total tare weight of 139ton. All vehicles were constructed on steel underframes with body framing of hard wood and coach sides of steel panelling. All cars were close coupled with standard emu jumpers carried on the cab ends, stencil headcode boxes were fitted. One interesting design feature with these units was that the driver's cab and guard's van were slightly inset, giving a tapered appearance to the MBS vehicle. Electric and control equipments were supplied by Metrovic and each motor coach was powered by two 275hp traction motors. In the guard's compartment a periscope was fitted whereby the guard could see along the roof of the train and the track ahead. These units were the first fitted with this equipment and after proving successful was carried forward into subsequent coach designs. After construction, the units

30
In pristine condition 4LAV No 2954 crosses the distinctive Ouse Valley viaduct near Balcome during the early 1950s, with a Victoria-Brighton service. On the back a 4SUB unit has been added to increase passenger accommodation.
British Railways

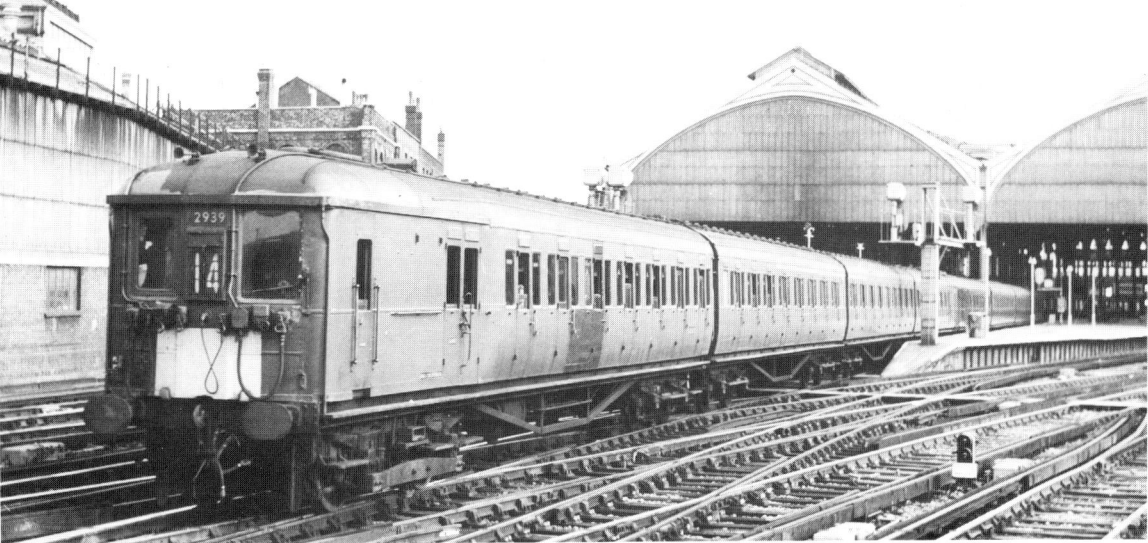

were put through their paces between Waterloo and Guildford via Cobham, but soon 12-car formations of 4LAV units could be seen on the Brighton main line, where 60min non-stop schedules could be kept with no trouble.

During 1939, construction commenced at Eastleigh works on two further units of the 4LAV design, these carrying running numbers 2954/5 and emerging during February/May 1940 respectively. These two sets in the way of equipment resembled the 2HAL units (described later), but the seating and internal layout was the same as the 1931/2 built units. The livery applied to all units when constructed was standard SR green, a livery in which the units remained until their withdrawal during 1969 — all units gained a yellow warning panel under the front windows from the early 1960s. After their initial testing on the South Western Division it was very rare to find these units operating off of the Victoria-Brighton/Worthing line.

31
A Victoria-Brighton slow service (headcode 14) arrives at Burgess Hill on 29 October 1968 after completing more than three-quarters of its journey from the capital. During the mid to late 1960s the majority of units were painted with small yellow warning panels, as displayed here on unit No 2949. *John Vaughan*

32
Departing from Brighton with the 17.28 stopping service for Victoria, 4LAV unit No 2939 leads a sister unit out from under the overall station roof on 5 September 1968, only a few weeks prior to the final withdrawal of the units. *John Scrace*

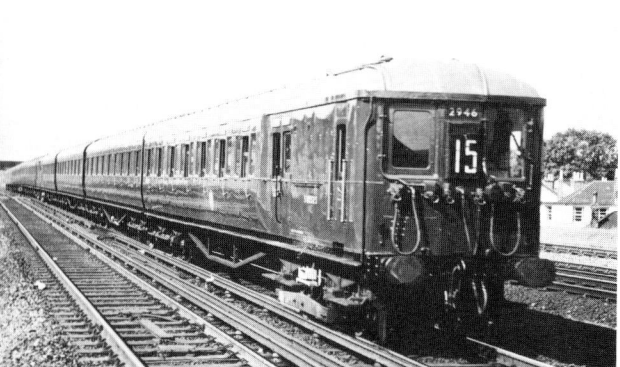

33
Approaching Norwood Junction 4LAV No 2946 in recently
ex-shops condition works a London-Brighton slow train
during the early 1960s. Roof mounted air horns were not
fitted at this time and warning of the train's approach was
given by a front mounted whistle situated to the right of the
driver's front window in this illustration. *P. J. Sharpe*

34
Traversing the beautiful Sussex countryside at Patcham
between Hassocks and Preston Park, two 4LAV units led by
set No 2928 operate the 14.28 Victoria-Brighton semi-fast
service on 27 April 1967. *John Scrace*

35
TC No S11512S stands with first class accommodation
nearest the camera. This vehicle, in common with all other
TC cars, was built with four third (later second) class
compartments and five first, but during the late 1950s three
of the first class compartments were declassified to increase
passenger accommodation. *G. M. Kichenside*

36
With steam water crane still surviving on the station platform and 4CEP unit No 7197 behind painted in Inter-City blue/grey livery, 4LAV No 2928 painted in SR green livery awaits to depart from Brighton with a semi-fast service for Victoria on 29 October 1968. *John Vaughan*

37
First class compartment of 4LAV stock, soon after construction, with SR rugs and plush upholstery. The carriage number 11518 (a TC vehicle) is transferred on to the carriage door along with the compartment letter 'D' indicating that it is the fourth first class compartment from the TCL coach. *British Railways*

PUL and CITY units

During 1932, the Southern Railway Company introduced 20 six-car main line units, each fitted with a Pullman car. The units were designed to operate express services between London-Brighton, and West Worthing. Construction was divided between the Railway's own works at Eastleigh, who constructed the trailer cars, and Metropolitan-Cammell Carriage Wagon & Finance Company/Birmingham Railway Carriage & Wagon Company Ltd who each built 20 driving power cars. Driving cars were of steel construction, and behind the driver's full width cab was situated the guard's compartment, which in these units contained emergency lighting batteries for half lighting, in the event of a main power failure, passenger accommodation was provided for 52 third class passengers. Traction equipment was mounted at each end under the driving car, and consisted of four 225hp BTH traction motors, together with a motor generator set which provided 70V power for train lighting; train heating was fed direct from the third rail and distributed through the train via 'power train lines'. Trailer cars were constructed of steel panelling on a hardwood frame. The internal layout of the trailer cars was: one with eight third class compartments plus half compartment (coupe) with four seats, and two cars: with five first class and three third class compartments. All trailer cars had end lavatories. The Pullman vehicle was provided by the Pullman Car Company who had 20 cars constructed by the Metropolitan-Cammell Carriage Wagon & Finance Company Ltd. The internal layout was of the composite type, with third and first class seating being provided, together with full cooking and pantry facilities. Power for the Pullman car was provided by a 20kW dynamotor which gave dc power at 110V. The livery applied to the units was standard SR green for all cars except the Pullman vehicle which was painted in standard Pullman colours. Unit numbering was 2001-2020 which was altered to 3001-3020 during the re-numbering of 1937. These 20 units were classified as 6PUL (six-car Pullman) units.

Three other Pullman units were constructed at the same time for use on the London Bridge-Brighton business services where a large number of City passengers required first class seating as well as a full on-board meal service. The three units built were classified as 6CITY, and emerged from the works during late 1932, closely following the 6PUL design, except that the three trailers were all equipped for first class seating, provided in seven compartments. Coach construction was carried out by the same manufacturers as for the PUL units, and traction equipment was of the same design. Unit numbers applied to CITY sets were 2041-2043 when built which were altered to 3041-3043 during early 1937. In common with Pullman Car Company practice all their cars within these 23 sets were named. The order of cars is given below (as at 1937) together with their names:

6PUL		6CITY	
2001 (3001)	Anne	2041 (3041)	Gwladys
2002 (3002)	Rita	2042 (3042)	Olive
2003 (3003)	Grace	2043 (3043)	Ethel
2004 (3004)	Elinor		
2005 (3005)	Ida		
2206 (3006)	Rose		
2007 (3007)	Violet		
2008 (3008)	Lorna		
2009 (3009)	Alice		
2010 (3010)	Daisy		
2011 (3011)	Naomi		
2012 (3012)	Bertha		
2013 (3013)	Brenda		
2014 (3014)	Enid		
2015 (3015)	Joyce		
2016 (3016)	Iris		
2017 (3017)	Ruth		
2018 (3018)	May		
2019 (3019)	Peggy		
2020 (3020)	Clara		

Normally PUL units would operate either singly or with a PAN set on the Victoria-Brighton/West Worthing route, while the CITY units would operate with a PAN on the London-Bridge/Brighton route. It was unusual to see these units in operation on other routes.

During 1964 4RES sets Nos 3054/5/6/7/9 were reformed and had their restaurant cars replaced by Pullman vehicles from withdrawn 6PUL sets and were reclassified as 4PULs operating on the Central Division for some four years.

38

Photographed during October 1931 outside the Metropolitan-Cammell Carriage, Wagon & Finance Company's works on what appears to be a makeshift track, motor coach No 11001 of set No 2001 awaits transfer to the SR at Eastleigh to be united with other coaches of the set under construction either at the SR works at Eastleigh or at the Birmingham Railway Carriage & Wagon works. Note the lined green livery applied. *Author's Collection*

39

Set No 2019 later to become 3019 still in comparatively ex-shops condition, stands in the sidings at Gatwick displaying the Victoria-Brighton line headcode. Pullman car *Peggy* built by the Pullman Car Company and manned by their staff stands third vehicle back. An interesting feature of this stock was that power collection was from both bogies on the power car. *GEC Traction Ltd*

40

From January 1937, the sets were renumbered in the 30xx series. Here set No 3005, formerly 2005 pulls away from Haywards Heath tunnel with another 6PUL set in tow on a Victoria-Ore working on 5 August 1955. The clips below the main rain strip were for roof boards, but these were seldom used. *British Railways*

41

Traversing the quarry line near Merstham 6PUL No 3016 forms a Victoria-Brighton fast service on 10 July 1955. The total seating on one of these PUL sets was for 72 first and 236 third (later second) class passengers, and were normally staffed by a driver, guard and four Pullman Car Company members of staff. *British Railways*

42
The motor coaches of these luxury main line units were designed by R. E. L. Maunsell and were of an all steel construction, internally finished in mahogany, with transverse seating divided by a central gangway. Here set No 3012 stands at Goring-by-sea station during May 1965 with a Victoria-Littlehampton train. *John Vaughan*

43
Comparison of designs: with 6PUL No 3005 on the left and 4LAV No 2943 on the right at Brighton station during the early 1960s. The London-Brighton and south coast line was always the stronghold for both these types of unit. *P. J. Sharpe*

44
Windows in the driving cars of these main line PUL units were of the balanced type and were designed to only open to a maximum of 7in, an amount considered suitable for adequate ventilation. Set No 3010 illustrated here travels towards Aldrington Halt near Hove while working a Victoria-Littlehampton via Worthing service on 31 May 1961. *C. P. Boocock*

45

Running under full power conditions a 12-coach formation of PUL stock heads for Brighton, near Haywards Heath, with a fast Victoria service on 25 August 1948. The motor bogies under the driving vehicle are each powered by two 225hp motors developing 1,800hp for a six-car set.
British Railways

46

6PUL unit No 3019 slows for the check at Clapham Junction on the down fast line, as it passes the now closed Clapham Junction 'B' signalbox on the right (closed during early 1981). The unit is operating a Victoria-Littlehampton service. *Frank Hornby*

47

To cater for the growth in first class traffic between London Bridge and Brighton three six-car Pullman units were introduced where all trailer coaches accommodated first class passengers. Illustrated here a 6CITY/6PAN formation approaches Haywards Heath with a Victoria-Littlehampton train on 8 August 1955. *British Railways*

48

Operating empty coaching stock (ecs) 6CITY No 3042 with Pullman car *Olive* as the fourth car back, approaches Crystal Palace (low level) while working from New Cross Gate to Victoria. *R. C. Riley*

49

Awaiting to depart from London Bridge, 6CITY unit No 3043 displays a Brighton line headcode when photographed on 9 April 1949. From 1947 due to reduced demand for first class accommodation two of the trailer vehicles were reclassified as composites giving two compartments in each coach to third (second) class passengers. *J. H. Aston*

50

The majority of PUL and CITY vehicles were withdrawn and scrapped during 1966, however some vehicles were reformed into 10 six-car sets and classified as 6CORs. These sets were intended for use in the SED, as a stop gap until other units were despatched to that area by new stock then under construction. Two six-car units formed of ex-PUL/CITY stock stand out of use at Lancing during 1968. *John Vaughan*

5BEL

The final three Pullman units to be built for the Southern Railway during 1932 were three five-car sets, constructed by the Metropolitan-Cammell Carriage Wagon & Finance Co, to all Pullman standards. The three sets, the first all electric Pullman multiple-units in the world, were designed for use on the new Southern Railway 'Southern Belle' service which was to commence operation between London (Victoria) and Brighton during 1933. The design of the cars was of the traditional Pullman type, with recessed inward opening passenger doors and distinct body styling. The formation of a five-car set was: Driving Motor Third seating 48 passengers, also accommodating a full width driver's cab and guard's brake; third class parlour seating 56 passengers; two first class parlours each seating 20 passengers, and another Driving Motor Third, giving a total seating throughout the set of 152 third class and 40 first class passengers. When introduced SR numbers allocated were: 2051-2053 which was changed during 1937 to 3051-3053. Passenger comfort was of prime importance when these units were constructed and to deaden internal noise levels, bodies were of all steel construction with floors in passenger areas insulated by cork, the majority of sides and most of the roof area was insulated by thick layers of 'Insulwood', with an air space between each. The external livery applied was standard Pullman car chocolate and cream, lined out in red and gold, with the Pullman Car Company coat of arms on each vehicle and the cab ends. In common with Pullman tradition all cars providing first class accommodation were given names, and those applied in these sets were: Hazel/Doris (2051/3051), Vera/Audrey (2053/3052), Mona/Gwen (2053/3035). The 'Southern Belle' name was not carried for many years as during 1934 it was changed to 'Brighton Belle' giving the units their famous 5BEL title. Operation of units was normally confined to the Brighton main line, usually operating as a single unit, but occasionally working in multiple with a 6PAN or 6PUL set. During early 1941 all units were taken out of service and stored for the war years, but regretfully prior to this, one unit did receive considerable damage at Victoria, which necessitated its return to its builders at the end of hostilities. Two units returned to traffic during 1946 and the third after repair in 1947.

Because of the lapse in service of some five years, when the majority of other main line stock was up for retirement during 1965, it was deemed that the BEL units were in satisfactory condition to operate for several years and were even given intermediate/refurbishing repairs at Eastleigh Works during 1969. The units emerged painted in standard BR blue/grey Pullman livery, and bearing the name 'Brighton Belle' painted on their now full yellow cab ends and coach sides. The stencil headcode was also replaced by the roller blind type. The final passenger run for the 'Brighton Belle' was on 30 April 1972 when many hundreds of well wishers joined passengers in biding farewell to these unique trains. After final withdrawal at Brighton Depot, the units were split up and cars sold individually, many seeing further use as restaurants or cafes, but deeming it impossible for a complete set to be seen together again.

51
Two 5BEL units led by set No 3053 operate over the quarry line near Merstham during the early 1950s. These three five-car sets must without doubt have been the most handsome emu stock to grace the tracks of the Southern, painted in distinctive chocolate and cream Pullman livery. *British Railways*

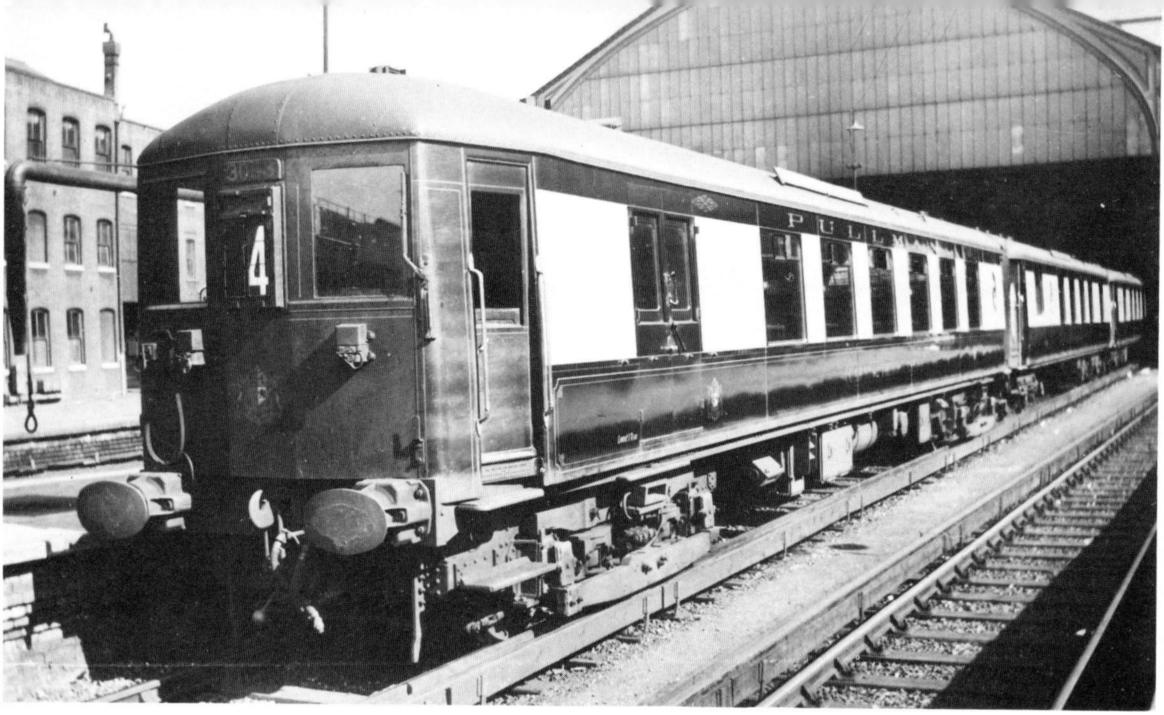

52
Close up showing detail of motor brake third Pantry No 92 of set No 3053, standing at Brighton, displaying the traditional London-Brighton headcode 4. The Pullman Car Company insignia will be noted on the front end under the headcode stencil box. *Les Elsey*

53
Rear three-quarter view of 5BEL motor vehicle showing the standard Pullman style inward opening vestibule doors on each carriage corner. Again on this stock a motor bogie with third rail pick-up was provided at each end of driving motor vehicles. *P. J. Sharpe*

54
In common with Pullman Car Company practice vehicles accommodating first class passengers were named, whilst those provided for third class passengers were allocated numbers. Here pullman car *Hazel* from BEL set No 2051 later 3051, stands in original as built condition with pantry and cooking facilities at the outer ends. *British Railways*

55

In original condition carrying its 20xx running number, BEL set No 2053 runs as a single unit near Copyhold Junction while working a Victoria-Brighton train during June 1935. At this point in time the vehicle class as well as number was applied under the saloon windows (just visible on the leading car). *Ian Allan Library*

56

Passing the 37-mile post near Purley a 10-car formation of BEL stock led by unit No 3052 heads for the sunny south on 3 July 1951. *British Railways*

57

Interior of third class saloon, with seating of a fixed style in a 2 + 2 configuration, with centre gangway. A unique feature in emu stock to the 'Brighton Belle' set was the clock situated above the compartment gangway door. The upholstery dates this photograph to the late 1930s. *British Railways*

58

Interior of first class BEL vehicle showing the plush lounge chairs formed in a 1 + 1 style. Each first class vehicle seated 20 passengers and contained a full kitchen compartment. The total weight of each first class vehicle was 43ton. Photograph taken in June 1939. *British Railways*

59
On very rare occasions would an enthusiast have the chance to capture a BEL train and a Class 24 diesel-electric locomotive in the same frame, but on 17 May 1964 the 11.00 Victoria-Brighton overtakes Class 24 No D5095 at East Croydon while working a Stevenage-Brighton special. *John Scrace*

60
Repainting of the BEL stock into standard BR Pullman livery of grey/blue was carried out at Eastleigh during 1969. As well as repainting, modern two-tone air warning horns were fitted on the cab roofs and roller blind headcodes replaced the older stencil type. Here 5BEL No 3051 approaches Clapham Junction on 10 April 1970. *John Cooper-Smith*

BRIGHTON BELLE

61
The individual coach names on first class vehicles gave way just to the train's name during the livery change of 1969; but at least the beautiful table lamps were not replaced by body mounted lamps. Headboard clips remained in situ but were not used from the mid-1960s. *John Scrace*

62
Official portrait shot of refurbished 5BEL unit, still retaining its stencil headcode. During refurbishing work, when the driving cars were painted with full yellow warning ends, the Pullman Car Company emblem gave way to the legend 'Brighton Belle'. *British Railways*

63
Looking rather forlorn standing in sidings at Brighton 5BEL motor cars with a 4BUF unit buffet car between await their final fate on 8 September 1977, standing alongside is 2BIL No 2090. All these vehicles were ready to take part in the Brighton Station Open Day held on 10 September.
C. Burnham

6PAN

The 1935 electrification of the Eastbourne and Hastings lines brought the construction of 17 six-car main line units — later to be classified by the SR as 6PANs. Unit numbers allocated were 2021-2037 which became 3021-3037 from late 1936. The 34 driving motor coaches were constructed equally between the Metropolitan Carriage, Wagon & Finance Company and the Birmingham Railway Carriage & Wagon Co Ltd, while trailer coaches were constructed in the railway's own works at Eastleigh. These units were basically the same as the 6PUL type, except that the Pullman vehicle was replaced by a first class trailer car fitted with a small pantry — for serving light refreshments, these PAN cars were normally manned and maintained by Pullman car company staff. The internal layout of the units was: Motor Brake open third seating 52, third class side corridor seating 68, first class pantry car seating 30, first corridor seating 42, a 68 seat third corridor and another 52 seat motor brake open third. One noticeable difference between these and the PUL units was the windows in the motor cars — which in the PAN type were of a fixed design with single air-stream ventilators above, these were of a new type used on the Southern, and were intended to give draught free ventilation. Control and power equipment were provided by the British Thompson Houston Co (BTH). The normal operation of the units was on the London-Eastbourne, Hastings, Brighton and West Worthing route — often working in multiple with a 6PUL or 6CITY sets. The livery applied was standard SR electric green, which was carried until the units were withdrawn or reformed during the 1960s.

During 1965, when many units were being phased out, various cars were reformed with PUL vehicles and entered service as 6COR sets, carrying numbers 3041-3050, being finally taken out of stock during 1969.

64
6PAN (six-car express pantry unit) No 3031 with pantry vehicle fourth from the front, heads for Earlswood on the quarry line near Merstham with a London Bridge to Brighton slow service on 11 July 1955. *British Railways*

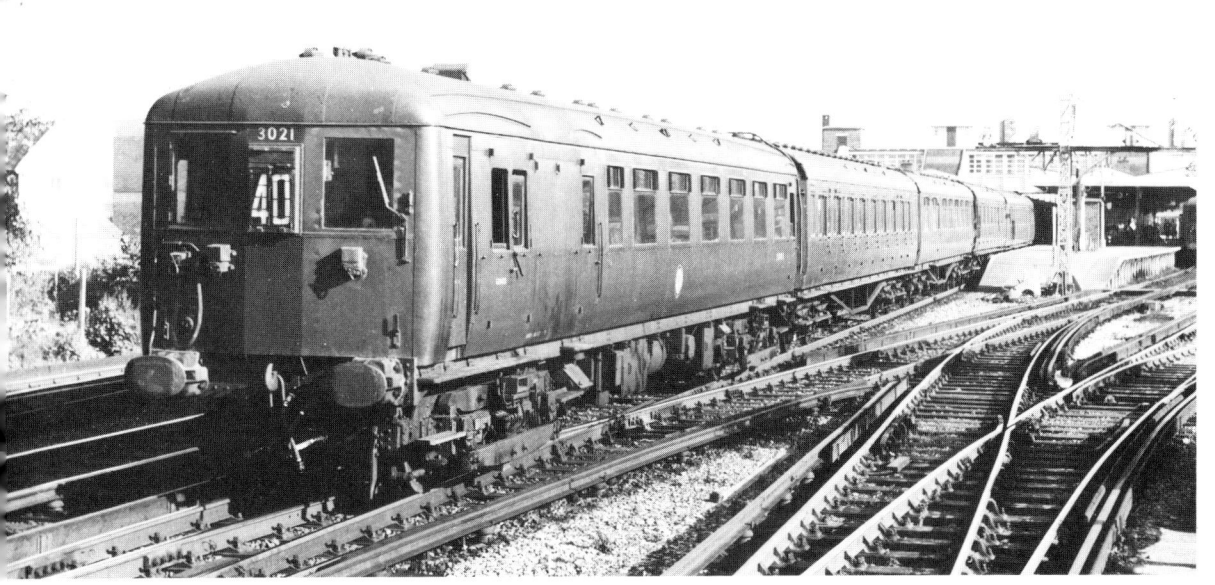

65
Externally the driving vehicles of PUL and PAN sets were only recognisable by their window design, on PAN vehicles sliding top lights were fitted in place of the balanced type used on PUL power cars. PAN set No 3021 illustrated here, departs from Horsham on 10 October 1965 with the 09.18 Victoria-Bognor Regis and Portsmouth Harbour train.
John Scrace

66
First class PAN (Pantry) vehicle from 6PAN set No 2030 later 3030, the pantry end being nearest the camera. The other part of the vehicle contained seating for 30 first class passengers. The livery applied in this photograph was brunswick green bodywork, black ends, grey roof with orange, cream and gold lining. *British Railways*

67
It was normal SR operating practice for PAN sets to be coupled to 6PUL units to form 12-coach main line trains. Here 6PAN/PUL formation with PAN No 3030 leading approaches Three Bridges with the 15.45 Victoria-Eastbourne/Hastings train on 27 March 1965. *John Faulkner*

68

With the bank holiday train reporting number (233) being carried in the fireman's side window, 6PAN No 3036 forms the 10.00 Victoria-Brighton train past Coulsdon North on Easter Monday 30 March 1959. *John Faulkner*

69

In 1935 ex-shops condition 6PAN No 2036 renumbered during early 1937 to 3036 in common with all other main line stock, runs near Pevensey Bay during proving trials. *British Railways*

70

In conjunction with special testing of electrical equipment the SR CM&EE commandeered two specially made up formations of 6PAN motor cars and 4COR trailer vehicles during the summer of 1964. Here the test formation led by SR electric locomotive No E5013 departs from Hither Green heading southwards. *S. Creer*

2 BIL

The first batch of 10 semi-fast main line units classified as 2BIL by the Southern Railway entered traffic during early 1935 for use on the Eastbourne line, each unit consisted of a Motor Brake Third, and a Driving Trailer Composite. Coach construction was again divided between more than one manufacturer, with five of the power cars being built by The Metropolitan Cammell Carriage Wagon & Finance Company and The Birmingham Railway Carriage & Wagon Co Ltd, while all trailer cars were constructed at the SR works at Eastleigh. The internal layout of motor cars was, behind the driver's full width cab there was a guard's/luggage brake van able to carry 1 ton of goods, followed by seven third class compartments connected by a side corridor, while at the inner end of the coach a toilet was situated. Driving Trailer cars were fitted out for four first and four third class compartments connected via a side corridor, an inner end toilet was also provided. At the outer end was a full width driver's cab. Traction equipment was carried at one end only, and consisted of two 275hp English Electric traction motors, with control equipment provided by the Metropolitan-Vickers Ltd. Underframes of the cars were of steel sections, while the bodies were constructed of steel panelling mounted on a hardwood frame. The total length of a two-car unit was 129ft 6in by 9ft 2in wide. Seating was provided for 24 first and 88 third class passengers. Unit numbers allocated when sets were constructed were 1891-1900 which were altered to 2001-2010 from 1937.

A further batch of units of the same general design were constructed by the SR at Eastleigh during 1936 for use on the Waterloo-Portsmouth/Alton routes, numbers allocated to these units were 2011-2048. Units carrying running numbers 2040-2116 were commissioned during 1937 and used on the Central section route to Portsmouth/Bognor Regis. During 1938 the final batch of units emerged from Eastleigh works numbered 2117-2152, these were built for the Waterloo-Reading route. The internal layout of these later built sets differed in detail from the original vehicles mainly in the motor car, where six first class compartments were installed together with a four seat coupe. On later built power cars control equipment was constructed by the English Electric Company. Units of the 1936 and subsequent builds were fitted with metal window surrounds, a vast improvement to the wooden surrounds fitted on the original units.

The livery applied to all units when constructed was standard BR green, and some units that remained in traffic until the early 1970s, when they were painted in standard rail blue livery. Two withdrawn BIL driving cars saw further use in trailer control set No 900. Further details of this are given in the relevant section.

71
Designed and built for use on the Central and South Western semi-fast services the 2BIL stock became the backbone of power on many routes during the 1940s and 1950s. Here set No 2026 formerly set No 1916 stands coupled to some 2HAL stock during 1940. *GEC Traction Ltd*

72
Descending from the high-level section of Portsmouth &
Southsea station and heading for Fratton, 2BIL No 2019
forms a rear portion of a Portsmouth Harbour-Brighton
'coastway' train during the early 1960s. The guard's roof-
mounted periscope can clearly be seen. *GEC Traction Ltd*

73
A superb period photograph taken at Reading (SR) of 2BIL
No 2114 being loaded with milk churns and other luggage
during January 1939. It is not often that illustrations of
these units are found with the bodyside destination boards
in use. *British Railways*

74
Running into Ascot station, the junction for the Aldershot
branch line, 2BIL No 2145 leads two other emus of the
same type on a Reading-Waterloo service during the
summer of 1938, soon after No 2145 entered traffic.
Semaphore signalling remained in use at this location until
the mid-1970s when the signalbox was closed and colour
light signals provided, being controlled from the modern
signalling centre at Feltham. *British Railways*

75
Passing a couple of superb SR lattice semaphore signal posts, 1938 built 2BIL No 2147 approaches Ascot station with a Waterloo-Reading train during the autumn of 1938. The stationmaster is standing on the platform observing this official photograph being taken. *British Railways*

76
For many years from the mid-1930s the Waterloo-Portsmouth & Southsea slow services normally detaching from an Alton train at Woking, were in the hands of 2BIL stock. As each coach of these units was provided with a lavatory, passenger comforts were cared for on the lengthy journey to and from London on a slow train. Illustrated here is set No 2121 arriving at Portsmouth & Southsea low level during 1957. *GEC Traction Ltd*

77
On two-car emu stock the traction equipment was always mounted on the bogie under the guard's brake van, in this case, it is in the form of two 275hp English Electric traction motors, motor resistances and other control equipment being mounted between the bogies. Set No 2064 in this illustration, nears Purley Oaks on 30 July 1966, with the trailer coach leading. *S. W. Stevens-Stratten*

78

The station enthusiast will not find this one shown in any railway atlas or publication, as it is really Christs Hospital station, near Horsham, renamed Longhampton for filming purposes. In the down platform 2BIL No 2150 forms the 10.36 Victoria-Bognor Regis train. Photographed on 13 March 1965. *John Scrace*

79

This interesting 1964 photograph shows Ash Junction, with the signalbox being demolished. The single line to the left once formed the Farnham-Wanborough connection which closed to passenger traffic from 4 July 1937. 2BIL No 2023 pulls around the tight curve and heads downgrade from Wanborough with a Waterloo-Guildford via Aldershot train. *P. J. Lynch*

80

With semaphore signals being the order of the day at Ford, a two 2BIL formation with unit No 2115 leading, operates the coastway service from Portsmouth Harbour to Brighton during 1968. *John Vaughan*

81

Displaying the Portsmouth Harbour-Brighton semi-fast headcode 60 a four-car train with 2BIL No 2054 leading approaches Angmering after covering 20 miles of the $45\frac{1}{2}$ miles coastway route. *John Vaughan*

82
Painted with a small yellow warning panel and a black diamond sign indicating guard's van and traction equipment at that end of the train, BIL No 2142 leads the 09.40 Bognor Regis-Victoria train out of Faygate on the Horsham-Three Bridges section of line. *John Scrace*

83
As mentioned in the introductory text to this section, some units remained in traffic to be painted in standard BR rail blue livery will full yellow warning ends. Set No 2062 was also fitted with roof mounted warning horns, and departs from Goring-by-Sea with a Brighton-Littlehampton train on 30 April 1971. *John Scrace*

84
Looking rather decrepit against the two 2BIL units in tow, 2NOL No 1826 converted from former LSWR steam stock at Eastleigh during 1934 leads the 10.02 Victoria-Bognor Regis towards Christs Hospital station on 6 June 1959. *John Scrace*

2NOL

The 2NOL (two-car non-lavatory suburban units) were first introduced during 1934 when units carrying numbers 1813-1890 entered service. Carriages for these sets were not new as all were converted from ex-LSWR steam vehicles at Eastleigh Carriage Works. Each two-car set was made up of a third class motor brake containing a full width driver's cab, a guards' brake/luggage van, seven third class compartments and a third coupé; and a Driving Trailer Composite providing three first and six third class compartments together with a full width driver's cab. The overall dimensions of a unit were 129ft 6in long × 9ft 2in in width, with a total weight of some 70ton. Passenger accommodation was 24 first and 135 third class, and the traction/control equipment was provided by Metropolitan Vickers.

During the rebuilding work many of the original LSWR fixtures and fittings were retained, such as door locks, air ventilators and luggage racks. The livery applied was standard BR suburban green.

Originally units operated on the Brighton-West Worthing route and were soon on the Horsted Keynes to Seaford and Ore line. By 1936 when the full complement of 78 units had been delivered, units took over the Western section suburban services from Waterloo to Windsor/Weybridge.

A technical point worth noting is that the final eight units (1883-1890) when converted were fitted with an electro-pneumatic control system. During 1942 several units had their traction equipment isolated and were operated as trailer sets — normally being marshalled with two 4SUB type units. An internal modification was carried out to most sets from 1943; this was the removal of the third class coupé in the Driving Motor brake coach and enlarging the guards' luggage van. After the cessation of hostilities during 1945 all the sets were returned to a powered status and units 1813-1850 returned to traffic with first and third class accommodation and were used again on Central Section lines, while sets Nos 1851-1890 became third class only — primarily for use on the Waterloo-Windsor line services. They finally ended their service during the mid-1950s, with many coaches giving their frames to 1957 built EPB/HAP stock.

Over the years these two-car suburban units operated over most of the electrified network on both suburban and main line duties, and proved to be some of the most reliable units built for their period.

85
Rounding the tight curve into Chertsey station on the Virginia Water-Weybridge line is 2NOL No 1872 during early 1936. When introduced these units, some of the first semi-fast stock to be constructed, were intended for use on the coastal services of the Central Section, but they soon found themselves operating on Western Section tracks, often on the Waterloo-Windsor/Weybridge line.
British Railways

86
Standing at Sydenham Hill with a Victoria-Sevenoaks train are two 2NOL units led by set No 1840 on 9 April 1959. In this view the guard's side lookout with small egg-shaped window can clearly be seen. *R. Lissenden*

87
An eight-car formation of NOL stock with set No 1867 leading, stands at Ashford station (Middlesex) while forming a Waterloo-Ascot race special during the early 1950s. The headcode 98 was only used for race specials on the South Western Division and it is this code that identifies the train from the usual stopping Waterloo-Windsor/Weybridge train. *D. J. Sutton (Ian Allan Library)*

4RES/GRI

To provide restaurant facilities for the 1937 Waterloo-Portsmouth electrification system, 19 four-car full corridor restaurant sets (4 RES) were constructed, to operate with the 4COR units (described in a later section). Each four-car set consisted of a Motor Brake Open Third at each end seating 52 passengers, being built at Eastleigh Carriage Shops. The external design of these coaches was new to the Southern as the driver's compartment occupied only half of the end section with a through passenger corridor in the centre, and a stencil headcode box in place of a second nose window.

The two trailer cars were both built by private manufacturers with the first class restaurant car being assembled by Metropolitan-Cammell and the third class vehicle by Birmingham Railway Carriage & Wagon Company. The internal layout of the first class restaurant was laid out for five first-class seating compartments each provided with four or six loose chairs, lavatory, and a dining area seating 12. The third class vehicle had a pantry, kitchen and dining section with seating for 36 passengers. Electric power for the cooking facilities was provided from the third rail or from a step-down dynamotor mounted under the car. The basic dimensions for a unit were 265ft 2in long, 9ft 8½in wide and 162ton in weight. Total passenger seating was for 42 first and 140 third.

After entering revenue earning service with 4COR units it was normal practice that units would be kept on the Waterloo-Portsmouth route, making occasional 'peak hour' trips to outer suburban areas such as Alton.

One 4RES unit worth special mention is unit No 3072 which was involved in a serious fire during 1952 which destroyed the restaurant vehicle, when rebuilt the coach was fitted out in cafeteria style and was reclassified as 4BUF.

These RES units all remained in traffic until early in 1962 when three were taken out of service and converted to Griddle sets, during which time the restaurant cars were rebuilt internally to contain a buffet saloon, a kitchen, and a bar section — the new Griddle car now seated 26.

Numbering applied to 4RES stock was 3054-3072, and the three converted 4GRI sets Nos 3056/65/68 were renumbered during 1964 to 3086-3088. The livery applied to units from new was standard BR green with several units acquiring yellow panel/nose ends during the 1960s.

88
Side detail of 4RES unit power car with the driver's cab and guard's brake (capable of housing 1 ton of luggage evenly distributed) on the left, and a saloon for 52 passengers travelling third class (second class from 1956) on the right. Equipment for power control and braking systems is mounted between the bogies. Illustrated here is car No S11149S of set No 3057. *P. J. Sharpe*

89
The stronghold for the RES stock was always on the
Waterloo-Portsmouth route, normally operating with one or
more 4COR type units. Here set No 3056 displaying the fast
Waterloo headcode nears Buriton between Rowlands Castle
and Petersfield. *British Railways*

90
Diverted from the main line due to a bridge renewal at Esher,
4RES No 3059 leads a 4COR unit past Hinchley Wood on
the New Guildford line with the 14.20 Portsmouth Harbour-
Waterloo service on 15 May 1955. *John Faulkner*

91
As mentioned in the introduction to this section, three units
during 1964 were converted to house a griddle car in place
of the RES vehicle, this was carried out due to the changing
needs for refreshments on main line trains. Here 4GRI
No 3086 leading 4COR No 3150 approaches Vauxhall with
the 13.20 Portsmouth Harbour-Waterloo train on
17 February 1968. *John Faulkner*

92
Interior of first class restaurant car in 4RES set with individual seats formed four per table in a 2 + 2 form. Individual light and attendance bell pushes were provided above each table. *British Railways*

93
Detail of power bogie as used under 4RES/GRI/BUF/COR units. The third rail collector shoe is mounted on a wooden shoe beam which is secured to the unit via brackets on the axle boxes. Above the centre of the shoe beam the springing can be seen with the shoe copper strip fuse mounted in a shoe fuse box at the top. In common with all SR emus the shoe fuse and bolts on the outside of the shoe beam are live all the time the unit is in contact with a third rail supply. *British Railways*

4/6 COR, 4BUF

4/6 COR

The 4COR (four-car main line corridor) sets were first introduced for the Waterloo-Portsmouth electrification in 1937. Sets were constructed at the SR carriage works at Eastleigh, and the front end layout contained a centre gangway with a side headcode, of the same design as fitted to the previously described 4RES stock. The formation of a four-car set was MBTO (Motor Brake Third Open) seating 52, a TC (Trailer Composite) giving passenger accommodation in five first and three third class compartments, a TK (Third Corridor) with seating in eight compartments and a single sided coupe, and another identical MBTO. Lavatories were provided in both trailer coaches at each end. The end gangways in the motor cars were provided for when units (up to three) were worked in multiple — giving staff and passengers access through an 8 or 12-car train — this also gave access to the restaurant vehicle for passengers travelling in the 'COR' portions of the train. After introduction units soon became known as 'Nelsons', this name was adopted due to their association with the Portsmouth line and the fact that with the headcode panel (stencil) fitted in place of the second front window, it gave the appearance that they only had one eye. Traction equipment was provided by Metropolitan Vickers in the way of four 225hp traction motors, two being fitted on each outer bogie of driving cars.

A second batch of COR units of the same design were constructed during 1937/38 when Eastleigh produced sets Nos 3130-3155, these were intended for use on the Mid-Sussex electrification scheme. Sets Nos 3156-3158 were introduced during mid-1940s and were formed of various new and some repaired war damaged coaches, from COR and RES stock. Units carrying running numbers 3159-3168 were introduced in 1965 by reforming various 4RES power cars and 4PUL/PAN trailers.

During late 1965 10 6COR units were formed of redundant 6PUL/6PAN cars, carrying numbers 3041-3050 these were CORs with a difference and they only had gangways within sets and a conventional full width driver's cab was supplied at each end. Dimensions of these six-car sets were 399ft 6in long by 9ft 3in wide; total weight was 250ton, seating was provided for 72 first and 256 second class passengers. After forming, units were seldom seen in use but during 1967 were used on summer relief services between London and the Kent coast towns.

The 4COR units after being displaced from the Waterloo-Portsmouth and South Coast route were used on outer suburban duties on the South Western and Central Divisions. They also became the regular power for the Waterloo-Reading, and Guildford via Ascot, and coastway services until their final withdrawal during September 1972.

From 1964 the restaurant cars were removed from six 4RES units and one 6PUL set, and after some reformation seven four-car corridor units entered traffic, classified 4COR(N) and numbered 3065-71. These units were normally used on the Victoria-Littlehampton and Worthing routes.

4BUF

To provide buffet facilities on the newly electrified Waterloo-Portsmouth route, a batch of 13 buffet car sets numbered 3073-3085 were constructed at Eastleigh during 1938. These units were of similar style to the 4COR units except that the trailer third vehicle was replaced by a restaurant buffet car. The internal layout of these buffet cars was laid out thus: service compartment, a bar with 10 stool seats and two toilets. The service compartment contained all cooking facilities, the power for which was supplied by an underfloor mounted motor generator. When introduced the buffet cars were painted in Malachite green while the remainder of the unit was in SR Brunswick green. An interesting feature of these cars was that there were no windows in the bar area and that the bar counter was concave in shape.

94
Painted with small yellow warning panel on its corridor connection 4COR No 3149 approaches Raynes Park on the up local line with a Portsmouth Harbour-Waterloo fast service during the summer of 1966. When this photograph was taken, the former stencil headcode had given way to the roller blind type. *B. H. Jackson*

95
Climbing towards Buriton Tunnel and passing Buriton Sidings between Petersfield and Rowlands Castle is a down fast Waterloo-Portsmouth Harbour train on 6 February 1955, formed with 4COR No 3113 leading. At this stage the roof mounted destination boards were still to be seen in use. *Les Elsey*

96
A 4COR/BUF/COR formation departs from Haywards Heath with the 09.28 Victoria-Brighton service on 31 May 1968. The 4COR/BUF units remained in use on the Brighton line until new 4CIG/BIG units were built at York during the 1960s. Passenger accommodation provided in a COR/BUF/COR formation was 1st: 90, 2nd: 520, Buffet: 26 compared with 1st: 126, 2nd: 544, on a 4CIG/BIG/CIG formation. *John Scrace*

97
Approaching Farncombe from Godalming, a Portsmouth Harbour-Waterloo train is led by 4COR No 3138 on a cold January day in 1965. The line to the left leads into Farncombe goods yard (now closed). *John Vaughan*

98
Due to Sunday engineering work between Guildford and Milford on 28 September 1968, services from Portsmouth to Waterloo were terminated at Milford where passengers were transferred to road coaches. Here 4COR No 3165 sets back clear of the crossover points at Milford preparing to return to the south coast. *A. Swain*

99
With new colour light signalling already in situ 4COR No 3143 hammers past West Byfleet signalbox with the 09.20 Portsmouth Harbour-Waterloo service on 24 February 1970, just a few weeks prior to the closure of the signalbox and full implementation of multi-aspect signalling.
John Scrace

100

Displaying all blue livery with BR double arrow logo, but still retaining the small yellow warning panel 4COR No 3152 stands in Wimbledon Park sidings on 2 September 1966. This unit was the first of the class to be painted in rail blue livery. *John Scrace*

101

Painted in BR blue with a full yellow cab end, 4COR No 3135 leads a 12-car COR/BUF/COR formation past Surbiton on 5 April 1969, with the 11.50 Waterloo-Portsmouth Harbour service. *John Faulkner*

102

During the late 1960s 4COR units replaced 2HAL stock on the majority of Waterloo-Reading/Guildford via Ascot services. In this illustration 4COR No 3119 crosses the River Thames bridge between St Margarets and Richmond with a Reading-Waterloo service on 23 August 1971. *British Railways*

103
One of the seldom used 6COR sets, formed of disbanded
6PUL/PAN coaches during 1965, stands dumped out of
service at Ford on 24 March 1969 awaiting its final fate.
About to pass by 2BIL No 2101 forms a Brighton-
Portsmouth coastway train.   *John Bird*

104
Framed by the road bridge arch at the south end of Guildford
4COR No 3167 slowly departs from Guildford station and
heads towards Chalk Tunnel with the 10.50 Waterloo-
Portsmouth Harbour semi-fast service on 26 June 1969.
John Scrace

105
With a 4CEP unit in the background a train formed of three
4COR units with set No 3167 leading, forms a London
Bridge-Littlehampton train on a July evening during 1970,
the train is seen at Elm Grove, near West Worthing.
John Vaughan

106
Slightly off the beaten track, 4COR No 3135 was used on a Locomotive Club of Great Britain 'North London Railtour' on 8 November 1970 and is seen here awaiting departure from Croxley Green. Note the centre rail which LT trains use, when en route to Croxley Green shed. *G. S. Cocks*

107
The driving and trailer composite vehicles of the BUF units were identical to those formed in the 4COR sets, the only vehicle that was different was the trailer third (second) which was changed to a Trailer Buffet. Here in this view of 4BUF No 3083, standing at East Croydon forming the 10.15 Saturdays only Victoria-Eastbourne, the buffet car is the third vehicle back. *John Scrace*

108
4BUF unit buffet car illustrated from the corridor side, in this June 1939 illustration the vehicle carries Southern Railway style lettering and would have been painted in SR brunswick green. In keeping with SR practice the carriage number 12523 carries no regional prefix or suffix and is carried near cant rail height. This buffet car was in unit No 3078. *Les Elsey*

109
A trailer composite coach as carried in 4COR and BUF units, is illustrated from the corridor side, with the five first class compartments nearest the camera, followed by the three third (second) compartments. *P. J. Sharpe*

110
Framed amongst the trees of Wandsworth Common 4COR No 3136 leads the 10.25 Victoria-Littlehampton service on 7 August 1965. The livery displayed on this unit is green with small yellow warning panel. *John Scrace*

112
Passing the substantial goods yards at Horsham, 4COR No 3127 leads a 12-car formation off the Dorking line and into the station with the 11.18 Victoria-Bognor Regis/ Portsmouth Harbour train on 19 July 1959. In the siding the three-coach branch train to Guildford awaits its turn in the station behind an 'E4' class 0-6-2T. *John Scrace*

111
Interior of Bulleid designed 4BUF unit buffet car showing the scalloping of the bar counter and wall ribs. The bar stools were fitted with revolving tops. In this view it is amazingly bright in the buffet bar area considering the dearth of windows. *British Railways*

113
During 1964/65 4COR sets Nos 3124/48 both exchanged one of their motor coaches for those out of a 6PUL unit, thus giving a non-corridor driving vehicle to each 4COR unit. To overcome operating difficulties caused by this unusual reformation, both units were normally kept coupled together (COR/COR) and operated on selected services only. Here the eight-car set stands at Surbiton with unit No 3124 together with former 6PUL coach S11034 from unit No 3017, leading. Both COR units reverted to their booked formation from June 1965. *John Faulkner*

114
4BUF set No 3080 traverses the single track section of the New Guildford line between Hampton Court Junction and Hinchley Wood with the 09.50 Waterloo-Portsmouth Harbour fast service on 6 December 1964. Normally the fast services from Waterloo to Portsmouth carried the headcode 80 or 81, but as this service was diverted the allocated headcode was No 6. *John Faulkner*

115
Taking the Portsmouth line at Woking Junction on 5 June 1970, 4COR No 3121 leads a 12-car formation on the 11.50 Waterloo-Portsmouth Harbour semi-fast service. On the right parked in Woking down yard is a Class 42 'Warship' which had failed the previous day. *John Scrace*

2HAL

The 2HAL (two-car half lavatory) main line units were intended for use on 1939 London-Maidstone and Gillingham electrification following construction at Eastleigh Carriage Works, but due to early delivery of some units, sets were used on other routes from early 1939. The formation of a set was DMT (Driving Motor Third), which together with its full width driver's cab and brake-van carried seven third class compartments and a DTC (Driving Trailer Composite) which had four first and four third class compartments, together with a toilet all connected via a side corridor. At the outer end of the coach was a small full width driver's compartment. Electric power and control equipment was provided by English Electric by means of two 275hp motors fitted with electro-pneumatic control equipment. The livery applied from new was SR green and the running numbers allocated were 2601-2676. The dimensions of a two-car set were 129ft 6in long × 9ft 2in wide, with a tare weight of 76ton. Total seating when built was provided for 32 first and 102 third class passengers in four a side seating in both classes, but this was altered to three a side in first class compartments during the early 1950s, giving a seating capacity of 24 first and 102 third. From the mid-1950s some units had one of their first compartments declassified, yet again increasing the third class passenger accommodation to 110.

During late 1939 Eastleigh Works started construction of a further 16 2HAL units, these were numbered 2677-2692 and entered traffic during early 1940.

Internal layout and traction equipment was the same as on earlier units.

Due to war losses six further units were constructed at Eastleigh during mid-1948, numbers allocated were 2693-2699. These units differed in external appearance and looked more like the suburban stock then under construction. Basic dimensions were the same as previous sets but the weight was reduced by 2ton. The internal layout was also varied but DTC cars remained unaltered while the DMT now had its seven third compartments connected via a side corridor, altering the seating to 24 first and 116 third class. The final 2HAL to enter traffic carrying running number 2700 emerged during 1955, resembling the 2693 fleet except that the DMT vehicle was now fitted out for seating in eight third class compartments with access via a centre gangway.

From their introduction until 1958, the units were used on the Charing Cross to Gillingham and Maidstone routes, when newly constructed 2HAP units took over, releasing units to operate on suburban and semi-main line duties on all three divisions until their final withdrawal at the end of 1971.

116
A 2HAL/2BIL formation with 2HAL No 2673 leading, slowly traverses the 20mph speed restriction out of Staines and approaches the Thames River Bridge with a Waterloo-Reading train during 1959. The motor vehicle is leading in this view. *J. C. Beckett*

117
Operating over the Maidstone route, the line that the stock
was built for, 2HAL No 2657 leads an eight-car formation
across the junction points and past the now closed signalbox
at Bickley Junction on 27 July 1955, while forming a
Maidstone-Victoria service. *Brian Morrison*

118
An official Southern Railway blacked out photograph of
2HAL stock, as used in advertising material for the
Gillingham and Maidstone extension schemes. This June
1939 illustration shows the unit from the trailer composite
end with the four first class seating compartments at the far
end of the leading coach. *British Railways*

119
After being displaced from the South Eastern Maidstone
route, these units became the regular motive power
along with the 2BIL stock on the Portsmouth-Brighton
'coastway' route. Here set No 2632 still painted in all green
livery, stands at Fratton on a Portsmouth-Brighton slow train
on 7 August 1957. *GEC Traction Ltd*

120

Front end layout of 2HAL stock, detailed equipment is also applicable to BIL, SUB, NOL, LAV, SL and WIM stock:
1. Eight-pin control jumper; 2. Power jumper receptacle; 3. Lighting jumper receptacle; 4. Lighting jumper cable; 5. Control jumper receptacle; 6. Power jumper (line volts); 7. Stencil headcode position; 8. Warning whistle; 9. Guard's periscope; 10. Coupling; 11. Main reservoir pipe; 12. Brake pipe; 13. Driver's safety device (DSD) isolating cock.
British Railways

121
The interior of a third class compartment of original HAL stock. The Southern Railway style lockable drop light window can be seen fitted in the door. The wall advertisements apparently contain one for Southampton Docks and a route map of the Southern Railway.
British Railways

122
Running past Goring-by-Sea signalbox and past the site of the long closed goods yard, 2HAL No 2659 leads a four-coach formation of HAL stock on a Brighton-Portsmouth working on 17 September 1966. The small yellow warning panel was added during the mid-1960s. *John Vaughan*

123
The final six 2HAL units were constructed at Eastleigh during 1948 to cover war losses, and these resembled the four-car suburban sets then under construction at the works. Here 4SUB look-a-like 2HAL No 2699 pulls into Angmering on the 12.52 Portsmouth Harbour-Brighton train on 30 April 1971. *John Scrace*

TC

The TC (Trailer Control) principle was on the BR drawing boards for many years and finally came into reality for the SR during the summer of 1963, when a rake of seven redundant emu vehicles were formed into unit No 900. The stock utilised to form this set were the two driving cars of withdrawn 2BIL No 2006 (with traction equipment removed), four 10 compartment trailers from various 4SUBs of the 4326 fleet, and one trailer composite converted from a trailer compartment third from 4SUB No 4115. The whole seven-car formation weighed 216ton and seated 72 first and 604 second class passengers. The overall length of the unit was 448ft $10\frac{1}{2}$in with a width of 9ft 3ins.

During September 1963 set No 900 took up passenger service on the 17.20 London Bridge-Tunbridge Wells West via Oxted train — a route and train where the unit was always associated. This unit also carried running number 701. Although this seven-car formation was usually referred to as a TC set it was unable to control a locomotive, and was in fact a seven-coach trailer set.

Following the basic success with the TC principle it was planned to convert coaches from withdrawn PUL/PAN units into six six-car TC corridor sets for push and pull working. As time came to prove only one set No 601 was marshalled, and was used only on its intended route (the Oxted line) for a short period from early in 1966 until being transferred to the Clapham Junction-Kensington Olympia service. Set No 601 was used on this line until being withdrawn following a collision. Accommodation in this set was for 72 first and 264 second class passengers.

For use with 'set' No 601 the SR converted a Class 33 diesel-electric locomotive No D6580, and fitted it with high level air and control jumper cables, from which control of the locomotive was transferred to the TC cabs, enabling the locomotive to stay at one end of the train but be controlled from the TC cab when formed at the rear of the train. Hence the term push-pull operation. This system was further developed and fitted into a fleet of 18 Class 33 locomotives during the mid-1960s. A fleet of 4TC units having their control by the same principle were also constructed for use with these locomotives on the Bournemouth modernisation programme of 1967.

124
After arriving from Clapham Junction, and having been controlled from the remote cab of 6TC set No 601, Class 33/1 No D6538 (33.118) stands idling at Kensington Olympia station on 5 May 1970, after operating the 08.46 service from Clapham Junction. This line was always associated with this unique TC train. *John Faulkner*

125
Front end detail of 6TC set showing the 27 wire multiple control jumper on the left and receptacle on the right, of the corridor connection. During conversion work the ground level air pipes were replaced by waist level fittings and an ETH (electric train heating) jumper (under driver's window on the right) was also fitted. *D. Simmonds*

126
If the Southern's motive power resources could not provide one of the region's 19 push-pull fitted Class 33s, use was made of a standard Class 33, but this was unable to be controlled from the remote cable of the TC unit. Illustrated here standard Class 33 No D6550 (33.032) hauls 6TC No 601 past the LTE depot of Lillie Bridge while en route from Clapham Junction to Kensington Olympia on 25 July 1969. *John Cooper-Smith*

127
The prototype TC set formed of seven redundant emu vehicles stands carrying the revised running number of 701 in Oatlands Cutting carriage sidings near Walton-on-Thames on 17 September 1967 while en route from Eastleigh Works to the Central Division. *R. Ruffell*

1940 Waterloo & City Railway stock

During 1938, the Southern Railway decided to modernise and recondition the Waterloo & City Railway. Apart from rebuilding much of the track and signalling equipment new stock was sought, and the English Electric Company of Preston were awarded the contract to construct 12 motor and 16 new trailer vehicles. These new tube sized vehicles measuring 47ft long, were equipped with air operated (guard controlled) passenger doors, and were fitted out to seat 40 passengers in motor cars and 52 in the trailer cars, with sufficient space for an equal number standing. Traction and control equipment was also supplied by the English Electric Company and carried at the 'Bank' end of each motor car in the form of two 190hp traction motors, all auxiliary and control equipment is mounted above the power bogie in an equipment compartment behind the driver's cab.

An unusual feature of the 'motor cars' is that they are fitted with a cab at each end, enabling them to run as a single car, but due to operating restrictions this is very seldom done and normally trains are formed of two motor coaches and three trailers between, or during slack periods two motor cars only.

When constructed, cars were painted in SR green with aluminium ends and doors, however in common with standard BR practice from the late 1960s cars have been painted in standard BR blue but retaining the aluminium or silver grey ends and doors.

Normally trains carry a letter A to E in the centre of the nose door, this is not for train reporting purposes but for local train identification. One non-standard feature of the line is that motor cars carry red lights at the front and back.

All regular and routine maintenance is carried out in the Waterloo & City Railway's own workshop, while classified and special work is normally carried out at Selhurst with the occasional visit to Wimbledon and Eastleigh.

128
Five-car train of 1940 Dick Kerr built Waterloo & City railway stock with motor coach No 56 leading, passes near Wimbledon on the East Putney line during April 1940 while on proving trials. *British Railways*

129
A complete five-coach formation with power car at each end
stands in the north sidings at Waterloo on 28 April 1950,
awaiting return to its home line via the hydraulic lift (situated
behind the train). Since this stock took up operating on the
line from 1940 it has become very rare for more than two
vehicles to be away from the line at one time.
C. C. B. Herbert

130
Power bogies of Waterloo & City motor vehicles are always
at the Bank end with associated electrical equipment being
housed in an equipment room above. Illustrated here is a
power bogie and third rail pick-up shoe. *British Railways*

131
To assist with train identification on the line, sets are referred to by the letters A to E, which are carried at each end of the train on squares affixed to the centre emergency door. Car S61 stands in this photograph at Bank station, with identification letter E on the front. *Author's Collection*

132
Waterloo & City Railway all steel trailer vehicles, each car is fitted with two pairs of double leaf sliding doors on each side, and an emergency inward opening end door. End connections on trailer coaches consist of air pipes and control cable sockets. This view of four trailer coaches was taken prior to the vehicles departing from the Dick Kerr works in Preston. *GEC Traction Ltd*

133
Standard five-car train with motor coach S58 nearest the camera standing awaiting departure from Waterloo. At all times these trains carry two red headlights and tail-lights indicating that electric and battery power is available. *Colin J. Marsden*

134
When not in use, or when undergoing routine maintenance vehicles are kept in the seven sidings provided at the Waterloo end of the line. Here motor coach No S61 stands on the points by No 1 siding, while making ready to re-enter service during the summer of 1980. *Colin J. Marsden*

135

Often during off peak periods (10.30-15.00) one of the sets operating the line is remarshalled to give a two power coach formation so releasing the trailer vehicles for maintenance. Standing in the driver's change-end siding at Waterloo on 26 August 1981 are two power cars Nos S58 and S62, which are preparing to run into the platform before forming a service to Bank. *Colin J. Marsden*

136

Amongst the apparent tangle of track and points in the sidings at Waterloo, a five-coach formation stands awaiting the shunt signal to be cleared before running into the platform to collect its passengers on 8 December 1979. *Brian Morrison*

137
The Waterloo & City Railway workshops at Waterloo are equipped to carry out most repairs including bogie replacement, but when the vehicles are due for heavy overhaul they are normally brought to the surface and taken to Selhurst repair shop. This is where car No S59 stands on jacks, in this 1980 view. *Brian Morrison*

138
To assist with a series of bogie changes that had to be carried out to the stock during 1980, various vehicles were taken to East Wimbledon or Stewarts Lane depots for attention. Car S56 in this illustration stands inside the East Wimbledon heavy maintenance shop on 18 August 1980. *Colin J. Marsden*

139
In connection with a series of CM&EE tests carried out on motor coach S58 during the late summer of 1977, the vehicle was brought to the surface and operated under its own power between Farnham and Alton. Here the vehicle awaits departure from Farnham on 27 September 1977. If it began to rain during these trials the car was soon taken out of service and placed under cover in Farnham Shed as it was not fitted with windscreen wipers! *Colin J. Marsden*

140
Interior of Waterloo & City Railway motor coach, showing the raised floor and seats at the far end which are mounted over the motor bogie. Note the Southern Railway covers to the coach ventilation louvres at the far end, each side of the equipment room door. *GEC Traction Ltd*

4SUB

The 4SUB (four-car suburban) unit was first born during the early 1940s when the SR carriage works at Eastleigh constructed a unit, carrying running number 4101, formed of four coaches, viz: Driving Motor Third, Trailer Composite, Trailer Third, and Driving Motor Third. The idea of these new four-car units was to eliminate the need for the trailer sets, and to run a complete service on suburban lines made up of four-coach powered units. It was also announced that many of the three-car suburban units that had a medium life expectancy were to be strengthened to four-coaches by utilising one of the coaches from a disbanded trailer set, while other three-car sets were to be augmented by adding newly constructed, second generation all steel trailers. Unit No 4101 with its first and third class accommodation entered traffic during late in 1941, being used on the Victoria-Orpington line. The basic dimensions for this 'new' unit was 257ft $4\frac{1}{2}$ins long by 9ft 3ins wide, with a total weight of 144ton; seating was provided when built for 60 first and 396 third class passengers, but as first class accommodation was dispensed with on suburban lines form 6 October 1941, it is unlikely that the first class accommodation was actually used and is most likely to have been declassified prior to entering traffic.

Some three years elapsed before the second SR 4SUB emerged, when during 1944 set number 4102 entered traffic, formed for all third class accommodation, but with one trailer of generous proportions, obviously intended for first class accommodation. This unit joined No 4101 on the Victoria-Orpington route until late in 1945 when it was used on Victoria-Tattenham Corner services.

The first production batch of 4102 type units started entering revenue earning traffic during early 1945 and carried running numbers 4103-4110 with a seating capacity of 468. The mass of reformed 3SUB units into four-car sets commenced entering traffic during 1942, when units numbered in the 1201 fleet were strengthened and became four-car sets in the 4131 and 4195 fleets. Later conversions from three to four car units were carried out during 1947-48, when 3SUBs of the 1658 fleet were strengthened with ex-LSWR 10 compartment trailers, and were renumbered in the 4172 and 4235 fleets. Units carrying running numbers 4250-4257 were reformed using war damaged three-car sets, and entered traffic during

1948-1949. The majority of other 3SUBs were augmented by adding new built second generation trailers of the same all steel design as the 4101 fleet 4SUBs. Eastleigh's construction of 'new' units carried on through 1946, when sets Nos 4111-4120 emerged, these had the unusual distinction of being built with wide compartment corridors in the motor cars, this was to accommodate the large number of standing passengers in leading vehicles during peak periods. A further batch of units to this design entered traffic during 1947-1948 and carried running numbers 4364-4377. Units Nos 4121-4130 were constructed during 1946 and were fitted out with a slightly revised internal seating layout. In place of the individual seating compartments, groups of three or four compartments were joined together by a centre gangway; this new arrangement gave more passenger freedom and increased standing room but reduced the total passenger loading to 382. After the introduction of this semi-open type stock, much pressure was placed on the railway authorities to only construct open or semi-open stock in the future.

When units Nos 4277-4299 entered traffic during 1948-1949 they were equipped with two eight bay motor cars with a centre gangway, a 10 compartment trailer, and a 10 bay trailer, giving three 'open' cars out of four. All units subsequently constructed were of the same design, with units numbered 4621-4652 entering traffic during 1949, 4655-4709 during 1950, and 4710-4754 during 1951. Some of the later built units were constructed as three-car sets and took their fourth vehicle from withdrawn augmented 3SUBs. Units Nos 4694-4699 and 4718 were equipped with roller blind headcodes, this was prototype equipment for use on the newly designed 4EPB units then under the advanced design stage. Many of the earliest augmented units were phased out of traffic as new 46xx and 47xx units entered traffic, and the majority were withdrawn by the late 1950s. Two 'new' units given numbers 4131/2 were formed during 1970, and were made up of withdrawn 2HAL motor coaches, with redundant all steel trailers between. Most of the 41xx and 43xx sets remained in service until the late 1960s and 1970s, when 1963 designed 4VEP and CIG type units displaced the 4EPBs and 2HAPs on to suburban duties. Most of the 42xx, 46xx and 47xx units remained in passenger service well into the 1980s, many being replaced by newly constructed 1972 type designed high-density Class 508 units. During the early 1980s the majority of compartment trailer vehicles were replaced by open trailers taken from withdrawn units, and several spare withdrawn trailers were rebuilt to EPB standards to augment two-car units to four, or to replace 4EPB compartment trailers.

The livery applied to all units when constructed was SR green, with many units of later builds being painted in standard BR blue from the late 1960s. During early 1982 66 units remained in traffic operating from Wimbledon Park and Selhurst Depots. In the autumn of 1982 set No 4732, the last 4SUB to receive a repaint, was outshopped from Selhurst painted in SR green livery with sunshine lettering.

As this book goes to press it has been announced that the few remaining 4SUB units will be withdrawn from May 1983.

141
Some of the first three-car suburban units to be converted into four-car units were the former 1201 series, most of which were augmented with former LSWR 10 or 11 compartment vehicles from trailer sets. Here in this rear three-quarter view of unit No 4227 formerly three-car unit No 1278, the additional trailer vehicle is the third vehicle from the camera. This unit was augmented during February 1945 and remained in service until June 1954.
British Railways

142
Nine compartment third (later second) class trailer built for 3SUB No 1300 but was later used in augmented unit No 4323. The additional vehicle No S10377 is at the far end of the picture and was one of a batch of newly constructed all steel trailers. *Ian Allan Library*

143
4SUB unit No 4506 augmented from 3SUB set No 1611 during 1948, departs on the down South Western Division slow line at Wimbledon on an Epsom train during the mid-1950s. Note the guard's side protruding sight position.
J. C. Beckett

144
4SUB No 4572 formerly set No 1696 augmented by an all steel trailer No S10452 during 1947, arrives at Surbiton on 3 September 1955 while working the 15.32 Waterloo-Guildford via Cobham service. *John Faulkner*

145
A somewhat unique unit was No 4590 which ran from May 1950 until July 1954, it was formed of two all steel vehicles and two of former LBSCR origin, giving the unit a most unusual appearance. In this view the unit forms the rear portion of an up train at New Cross on 6 April 1953. After July 1954 the all steel driving vehicle No S12664 was formed in to the new 2HAL No 2700. *R. C. Riley*

146
Three-car suburban all steel unit No 4285 introduced during 1948-9. This unit forming one of a batch of 34 were the first 4SUB units to be built with centre gangway driving vehicles to try and alleviate some of the overcrowding which previously occurred in narrow compartments. In this illustration unit No 4285 was photographed near Shortlands during 1959 on a Victoria-Orpington train.
GEC Traction Ltd

147
All steel compartment trailer for 4111-4120 4SUB fleet
under construction in the carriage works at Eastleigh during
1946. The two vertical semi-circular recesses above the
door drop light window were air intakes for coach
ventilation. *British Railways*

148
1946 built 4SUB No 4127 in pristine condition carrying
'Southern' legend above the running number. Motor coaches
of this batch of units Nos 4121-4130 were built with two
groups of four compartments, each with a central
gangway. *H. M. Madgwick*

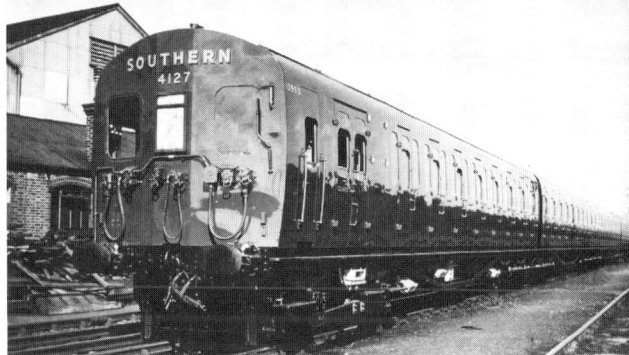

149
Joining into the New Guildford line at Effingham Junction
two 4SUB units form a London Bridge-Effingham train on
2 April 1955. The leading unit No 4190 was formerly 3SUB
No 1790 which was strengthened to four coaches during
November 1946 by the addition of one-coach of trailer set
No 1078. The rear unit in this illustration is an all steel 1948
build set. *John Faulkner*

150
4SUB No 4504 formed of LBSCR stock, passes Wimbledon West freight yard on 19 April 1957, while heading the 10.53 Waterloo-Hampton Court train. The two electrified tracks in the foreground are the Central Division Sutton lines. *John Faulkner*

151
1948 Eastleigh works built all steel 4SUB No 4647 pulls out of Knockholt tunnel with a down Cannon Street-Sevenoaks service on 10 May 1952. At this point in time the applied livery was standard SR green with yellow BR emblem and numerals. A warning whistle is mounted to the right of the driver's window. *R. E. Vincent*

152
Following collision damage at Norwood Junction on 31 December 1968 No 4103 had its power coach No S10946 written off as being uneconomical to repair. At the same time following the withdrawal of some of the HAL stock, motor coach No S10762 formerly of HAL No 2644 was spare and took up one of the motor coach positions in SUB No 4103. The unit is seen here with HAL end leading at Raynes Park on a Waterloo-Waterloo roundabout service. *John Faulkner*

153
The majority of 4SUB units were built with a stencil headcode, but a handful were fitted with various early roller blind systems, displayed here on unit No 4721 on the right. Units fitted with stencil headcodes were equipped with a stencil frame, a complete set of numbers 0–9 and a black blank. No double number codes were used so only one set of numerals were necessary at each end. Units Nos 4628/4721 in this illustration stand in Durnsford Road sidings on 28 February 1967. *R. Ruffell*

154
Under BR's numerical emu numbering policy the 4SUB units were classified as 405 which, from the 1970s, was displayed along with the maintaining depot on the unit front end. Unit No 4630 carrying WD (Wimbledon) shed code stands in the reception siding of its home shed on 18 August 1980. *Colin J. Marsden*

155
With the Southern Railway designed Surbiton station in the background an 8SUB formation with unit No 4641 leading departs from the up local platform of the station with the 09.44 Hampton Court-Waterloo train on 4 April 1980. *Colin J. Marsden*

156
One of the strongholds for the SUB units has always been Clapham Junction, where the enthusiast can observe both South Western and Central units from one vantage point. Illustrated here unit No 4626 departs from Clapham Junction with a Waterloo-Chessington train on 9 October 1980. The ornate former station entrance buildings behind the second and third coaches were destroyed by fire during the summer of 1981. *Colin J. Marsden*

157
After the introduction of 1972 design Class 508 high density emus on selected SWD routes during 1980, these 'old ladies of the road' were displaced to mainly peak period operation, but remained on regular use on Waterloo-Hounslow-Twickenham, and Waterloo-Dorking-Horsham services due to clearance problems on Class 508 units, until 1982. 4SUB No 4645 illustrated here approaches West Barnes Lane crossing with the 08.42 Waterloo-Dorking service on 5 May 1981. *Colin J. Marsden*

158
So as to provide a balanced working for units, not all trains return to their maintenance depot at the end of each day's work, therefore various stabling and servicing shed are provided throughout the region. One of these is situated at Effingham Junction where unit No 4618 was photographed during the night of 21 October 1980. *Colin J. Marsden*

159
With Class 73/1 electro-diesel No 73.102 in the background 4SUB No 4657 displays the Waterloo-Windsor headcode while stabled overnight at Waterloo during the early hours of 22 April 1981. *Colin J. Marsden*

160
Due to coupling incompatibility SUB stock is unable to operate in multiple with any other powered passenger stock now in traffic on the SR. Illustrated here a single unit No 4654 trundles through the trees lined cutting between Surbiton and Berrylands with the 09.44 Hampton Court-Waterloo service on 17 May 1980. *Colin J. Marsden*

161
To save conflicting moves in the Wimbledon area during the late morning peak period several empty coaching stock trains from Waterloo to Wimbledon Park Depot are routed via the suburban branch line terminating at Chessington or Hampton Court. Bound for Wimbledon depot and carrying the universal 'To Wimbledon Park Depot' headcode an 8SUB formation led by unit No 4639 approaches Surbiton after running from Waterloo via Hampton Court.
Colin J. Marsden

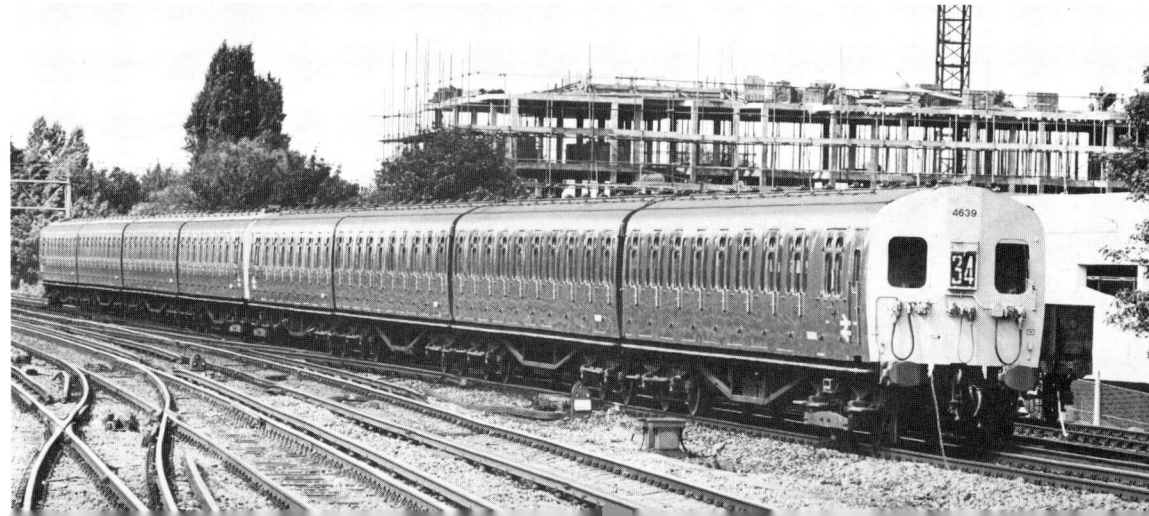

162
4SUB cab layout: **1** Westinghouse brake valve; **2** Master switch FOR/REV; **3** Power handle; **4** Horn valve; **5** Window wiper valve; **6** Window wiper manual handle; **7** Motor trip/set switch; **8** Brake pipe isolating key. *Colin J. Marsden*

163
Prior to the introduction of Class 508 units on suburban services 4SUB No 4664 approaches New Malden with the 10.46 Waterloo main-Waterloo-Windsor roundabout service. On the left can be seen some severe 'wet patches' on the up through line caused by the heavy axle loading of the Class 430 (REP) units. *Colin J. Marsden*

164
Many Central Division suburban services are also operated by 4SUB units, here seen passing the carriage sidings at Streatham Hill, used to stable suburban and main line units during off peak periods, is No 4291 forming a Victoria-Beckenham Junction train on 5 March 1981.
Colin J. Marsden

165

During the summer of 1980 following the introduction of Class 508 units many SUB units were withdrawn or stored. To bring the remaining operative set into line with modern operating requirements TSO (Trailer Second Open) vehicles in withdrawn sets were exchanged for TS (Trailer Second) compartment vehicles in service units to form sets of all open seating. Unit No 4655 passes under the road bridge at Wimbledon on 5 May 1981 with a Waterloo-Dorking service. *Colin J. Marsden*

166

Running in far from ideal conditions set No 4670 makes headway from Surbiton on 24 January 1979 with an early morning Hampton Court-Waterloo train. In bad and icy conditions many drivers prefer to have a SUB unit under their control, as with motors under each driving position, and no fancy electrical protective devices to cause trouble, they consider progress is more rapid. *Colin J. Marsden*

167

During 1982 the SR Management decided that the final Class 405 (4SUB) to receive a repaint, No 4732, would be outshopped in SR green with sunshine 'Southern' lettering. However to conform to present safety requirements it was necessary for the unit to have a full yellow warning end. Set No 4732 shunts towards Selhurst's washing machine during October 1982. *Colin J. Marsden*

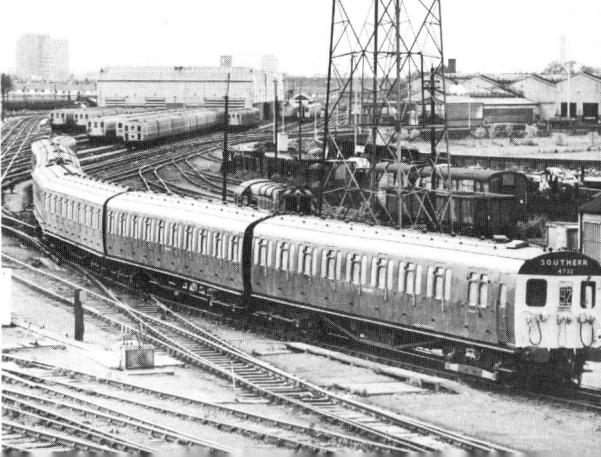

168
Many units that have been withdrawn during the early 1980s were sent to Horwich Works on the LMR for scrapping and possible conversion of some trailers to EPB standards. Here passing Manchester Victoria set No 4647 forms part of a freight train bound for the works on 16 September 1980. *Richard Fox*

169
Old Meets New: 4SUB No 4621 stands alongside one of its interim replacement units of Class 508, which will remain on the SR until the purpose built Class 445s are ready for delivery. This photograph was taken outside the CM&EE depot at Strawberry Hill on 10 May 1980. *Colin J. Marsden*

170
Standing under the fluorescent strip lighting of London's Waterloo station set No 4656 awaits its passengers for the 18.42 Waterloo-Dorking service on 20 October 1980. *Colin J. Marsden*

171
Basking in the warm summer sun by the wooden platform at Hampton Court set No 4659 waits to follow the booked passenger service to Waterloo with empty coaching stock bound for Wimbledon Park. All basic unit data ie weight, length and width can be seen stencilled on the front end under the route learner's window. *Colin J. Marsden*

172
A Hampton Court bound service passes between Raynes Park and New Malden on 18 May 1980 while forming the 16.56 service from Waterloo. *Colin J. Marsden*

4 DD

An interesting innovation was placed on the drawing boards of the Southern Railway just prior to nationalisation in 1948. This was the 'Double-Decker' train, designed at the SR carriage works at Eastleigh by O. V. S. Bulleid. This experimental design had passenger accommodation on two levels, but unlike a bus, seating was arranged 'high' and 'low' through the train, with a few shallow steps leading to the higher seating areas.

The first DD unit to emerge, did so during late 1949 and was based on the by then well proven 4SUB design. Passenger reaction was not all that welcoming, as people soon filled the lower deck and were standing, while seats were still available on the upper deck. In a four-car unit some 552 passengers could be seated, with sufficient room for another 150 standing. Thus giving, when the two units were coupled together, a train capable of moving some 1,404 passengers. Due to operating restrictions the two units normally worked coupled together and were used exclusively on the South Eastern route from Charing Cross to Dartford, and due to loading restrictions no external stepboards were provided, and as a result some passenger accidents resulted. The running numbers applied were 4001 and 4002, and the livery carried was standard BR green, which was later changed to standard BR blue during the late 1960s.

Running numbers were also altered so as to give the 40xx range to the SR's new breed of suburban emu; the 4DDs were renumbered on 18 November 1970 to 4901 and 4902. The general dimensions for a train were: 257ft 5in long by 9ft 3in wide, with a total tare weight of 133ton. The internal layout of driving cars was laid out for 55 high level and 55 low level passengers, while in trailer coaches 66 high level and 78 low level seats were provided. In addition to these each car had 10 tip-up seats provided on the high level. All traction and control equipment was supplied by the English Electric Company. One interesting item in these units was the fitting of strip lighting and pressure ventilation, the latter was necessary as on the high level all windows were of the fixed style — due to limited clearances. Westinghouse non self lapping electro-pneumatic brakes were also fitted. The DD units made their final passenger run between Charing Cross and Dartford via Bexley on 1 October 1971 and following this all cars were withdrawn with the majority being sent for scrap.

173
Ugly but attractive is perhaps one way to describe these DD units. As can be seen from this view of set No 4001 pulling out of Haywards Heath tunnel on a trial run during the summer of 1949, these units were based on the 1940s build of all steel suburban stock. *British Railways*

174
Due to restricted clearances the DD sets were confined to use on the Charing Cross or Cannon Street-Gravesend route. Here displaying green livery with full yellow ends set No 4002 awaits to depart from Charing Cross with an evening service bound for Dartford via Bexleyheath. *British Railways*

175
Interior view showing lower seating deck with stairs to upper deck in the foreground. Each motor coach contained five lower and five upper deck seating areas each level seating some 55 passengers plus additional tip-up seats by the steps. *British Railways*

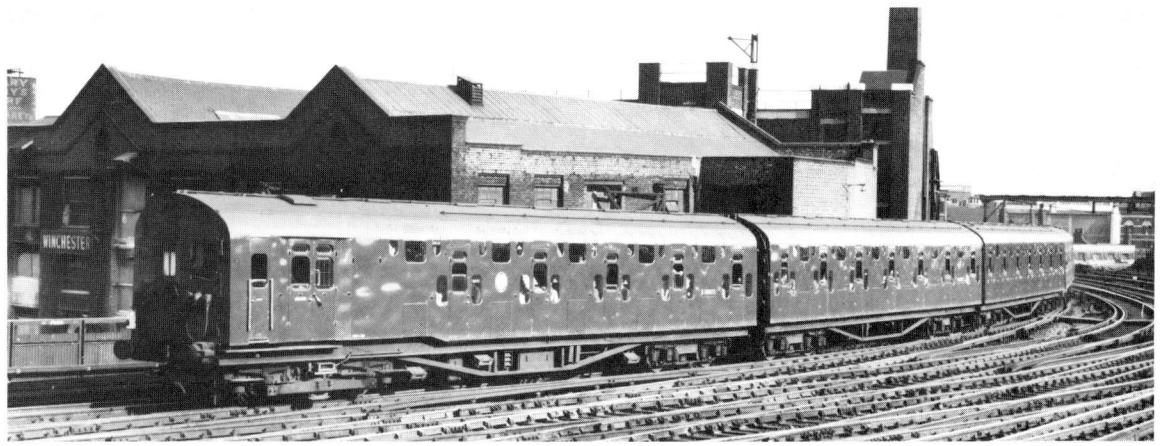

176
Side view showing external detail of motor coach and
adjoining trailer. It will be seen that no external stepboards
were provided on this stock, except at the driver's and
guard's position, this was due to the vehicle body being of
9ft 3in and the additional width of a stepboard would have
brought the units completely outside the British loading
gauge. In this view unit No 4002 approaches Cannon Street
on 12 June 1959. *R. C. Riley*

177
Approaching London Bridge and slowing for the station stop
4DD units Nos 4002/4001 form the 16.23 Gravesend-
Charing Cross train on 29 April 1954. Both of the DD units
were fitted with roller blind route indicators from new.
R. C. Riley

178
An unusual feature of both units was the fitting of a non-self lapping electro-pneumatic brake, again rendering them as non-standard. The two jumpers on the nose end are for power and control. This rear three-quarter view was taken at Waterloo East on 12 May 1969. *John Bird*

179
So as to vacate the 40xx numbering series in readiness for the SR new suburban emus, both DD sets were renumbered in the 49xx range during 1970. After operating over the same route for some 20 years the sets were withdrawn from passenger service after the arrival of the 18.04 Charing Cross-Dartford on 30 September 1971. In this illustration set No 4901 awaits its final fate dumped in sidings at Plumstead on 7 October 1971. *John Scrace*

4 EPB early design

The direct descendant of the 4SUB type stock described in an earlier section was the 4EPB (four-car suburban fitted with an electro-pneumatic brake). These sets, similar in appearance to the SUB type, were tentatively planned prior to 1948 and thereby have to be touched upon in this volume, but did not enter traffic until December 1951 on trial running on the New Guildford line. The main differences in these sets from the 4SUBs was the front end design and in the power/control equipment. The driver's cab had no side access doors and entry was via the adjacent guard's van, the driving position was of a more modern and pleasing appearance with all controls and relevant equipment situated on a 'surround desk'. The external design of the cab was also altered, as a buckeye coupling with a Pullman style rubbing plate were fitted, together with the high (waist) level multiple control cables and brake pipes, enabling staff to couple units for multiple operation without working at track level. The headcode system fitted was of the two character roller blind type. Braking systems fitted to units were supplied by The Westinghouse Co Ltd in the form of an electro-pneumatic system incorporating the auto air brake for emergency use. Power for all control/EP braking/ and train lighting was supplied at 70V from a motor generator (MG) with back-up power being provided by a battery both of which were housed under the sole bar on the motor cars.

The formation of units was Motor Brake Open/ Trailer Third Open/Trailer Third/Motor Brake Open; all the cars were built at Eastleigh and were of steel construction. Several compartment trailers were converted from second generation 4SUB vehicles. The livery that applied to the units when constructed was SR green, which was changed during the late 1960s to BR rail blue. During the 1980s the majority of units still remained in regular service and many now sport two-tone Inter-City livery. Sets were constructed for suburban duties and have worked these services for most of their lives, however for some years units operating on the Central and Western Sections have been used for outer-suburban and main line duties during peak periods.

Running numbers allocated were 5001-5053, 5101-5260, and under the BR standard numerical classification the units became Class 415.

During 1981 many units of this class have been passing through works for general/refurbish repairs, giving these 25 year plus servants a further lease of life.

180

As mentioned in the introductory text to this section the basic EPB (electro pneumatic brake) fitted units have been lightly covered in this volume as these units were planned prior to 1948. In passenger accommodation these units were no different to the SUB stock but technically there were some large advances namely the fitting of a 70V motor generator set for control purposes, re-designing the cab layout and installing an EP brake system, and the fitting of buckeye coupling and rubbing plates with high level air and control pipes. Illustrated here the first unit carrying an S prefix to the 5001 running number nears Claygate on 17 December 1951 on proving trails. *British Railways*

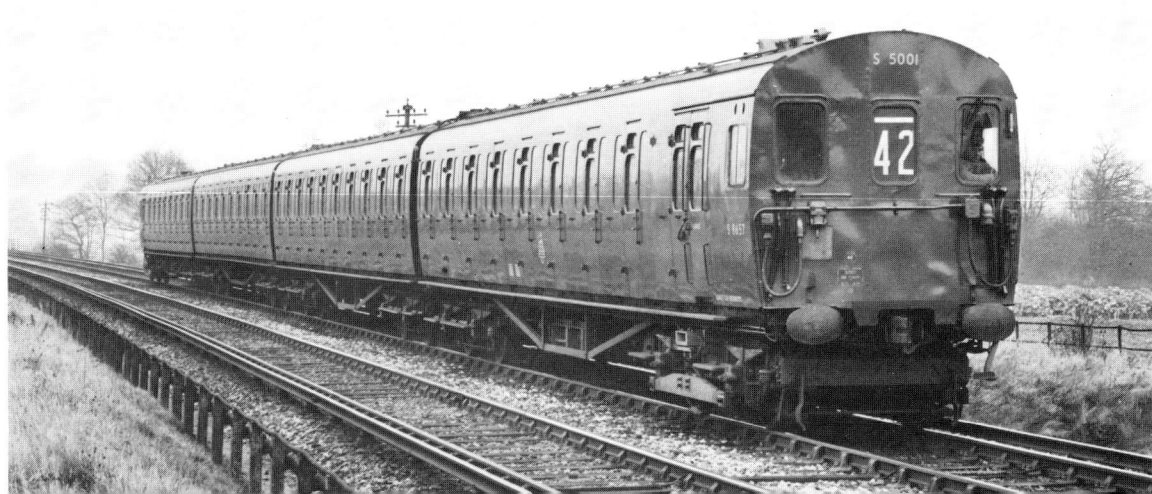

181

A superb 1957 view of Hampton Court showing SUB and EPB type units in the station area. Due to the incompatibility of most electrical and control systems these two types of suburban units were unable to operate together. On the right of the view is the now closed and pulled down Hampton Court Goods shed. *British Railways*

182

Cab layout provided in EPB style units: **1** Brake valve; **2** Window wiper control valve; **3** Meter light switch; **4** Cab light switch; **5** Route indicator light switch; **6** Duplex gauge (brake pipe/main reservoir); **7** Brake cylinder gauge; **8** Air horn valve; **9** For/Rev switch; **10** Power handle; **11** Driver's switch key (EP key); **12** Master switch; **13** Ampmeter; **14** Motor overload reset button; **15** EP brake indicator light (green); **16** Line indicator light (red); **17** Motor generator running indicator light (white); **18** AWS reset button; **19** AWS sunflower indicator; **20** Cab to cab loundaphone; **21** AWS isolation cock. *Colin J. Marsden*

183

Suburban Miscellany: In the foreground a 'modern' suburban 1951 built EPB unit approaches Wimbledon West with a London Bridge-London Bridge roundabout service while in the background an 8SUB formation awaits the signal to pull into Wimbledon Station with a Hampton Court-Waterloo rush hour train on 5 May 1981. *Colin J. Marsden*

Construction data

Type	Original numbering	Re-numbering	Year introduced	Car type (as built)	Notes
WC	1-17*		1898-9	M ⎫	Original Waterloo & City Railway
WC	21-36*		1898-1922	T ⎬	stock
WC	51-58*		1940	M ⎫	Waterloo & City Railway
WC	71-86*		1940	T ⎬	Replacement stock
SL	†		1909	MBT/TF/MBT	Later converted to two-car sets
CP	†		1911-1914	MBT/DTC/DTC	
CW	†		1923-1924	DTT/DTC/MLV/TC/DTT	
—	E1-E84	1201-1284	1914-1917	MBT/TC/MBT	LSWR motor sets
—	989-1000		1937-1938	T	Formed 1 LSWR/1 LBSCR coach
—	1001-1024		1919-1922	T	Two former LSWR coaches
—	1025-1037		1925	T	Two former LBSCR coaches
—	1038-1050		1935-1936	T	One LSWR/1 LBSCR coach
—	1051-1117		1925-1926	T	Two former LBSCR coaches
—	1118-1120		1937	T	1 LSWR/1 LBSCR coach
—	1121-1167		1928-1929	T	1 SECR/1 LSWR coach
—	1168-1187		1929-1930	T	Converts from CP stock
—	1188-1194		1930-1931	T	1 SECR/1 LSWR coach
—	1195-1198		1934-1935	T	Two former LSWR coaches
—	1199-1200		1937-1938	T	1 LSWR/1 LBSCR coach
3SUB	1285-1310		1925	MBT/TC/MBT	Short frame sets
3SUB	1401-1495		1925	MBT/TC/MBT	Former SECR steam stock
3SUB	1496-1524		1925	MBT/TC/MBT	Long frame sets
3SUB	1525-1534		1926	MBT/TC/MBT	Former SECR steam stock
3SUB	1579-1584		1937	MBT/TC/MBT	Former LSWR steam stock
3SUB	1593-1599		1934	MBT/TC/MBT	Former LSWR steam stock
3SUB	1601-1630		1927-1928	MBT/TC/MBT	Former SECR steam stock
3SUB	1631-1657		1927-1928	MBT/TC/MBT	Former LBSCR steam stock
3SUB	1658-1701		1927-1928	MBT/TC/MBC	Former LSWR steam stock
3SUB	1702-1716		1927-1928	MBT/TC/MBC	Former LBSCR steam stock
3SUB	1717-1772		1928-1930	MBT/TC/MBC	Former LBSCR ac electric stock
3SUB	1773-1785		1930	MBT/TC/MBC	Former LSWR steam stock, some mounted on former ac underframes
3SUB	1786-1796		1931	MBT/TC/MBT	Former LSWR steam stock
3SUB	1797-1801		1932	MBT/TC/MBT	Former LBSCR steam stock
2SL	1901-1908	1801-1808	1929	MBT/DTC	Rebuilds from former SL ac cars
2WIM	1909-1912	1809-1812	1930	MBC/DTT	Rebuilds from former SL ac cars
4LAV	1921-1953	2921-2953	1931-1932	MBT/TC/TCL/MBT	
4LAV	2954-2955		1940	MBT/TC/TCL/MBT	
6PUL	2001-2020	3001-3020	1932	MBTO/TTK/TC/TCP/TC/MBTO	
4PUL	3054/57/59		1964	MBO/TFK/TCP/MBO	4RES unit with TRT car removed and replaced by PUL vehicle
6CITY	2041-2043	3041-3043	1932	MBTO/TFK/TFK/TCP/TFK/ MBTO	
5BEL	2051-2053	3051-3053	1932	MBTP/TSP/TFP/TFP/MBTP	
6PAN	2021-2037	3021-3037	1935	MBTO/TSK/TFK/TFK(P)/TSK MBTO	
2BIL	1891-1899	2001-2010	1935	MBTL/DTCL	
2BIL	1901-1920	2011-2030	1936	MBTL/DTCL	
2BIL	1954-1971	2031-2048	1936	MBTL/DTCL	
2BIL	2049-2152		1937-1938	MBTL/DTCL	

Type	Original numbering	Re-numbering	Year introduced	Car type (as built)	Notes
2NOL	1813-1890		1935-1936	MBT/DTC	
4RES	3054-3072		1937	MBTO/TFK/TRT/MBTO	
4COR	3065-3071		1964	MBSO/TFK/TSK/MBSO	Former 4RES units with 6PAN, TCK's in place of TRT vehicle
4COR	3101-3155		1937-1938	MBTO/TTK/TCK/MBTO	
4COR	3156-3158		1948	MBTO/TTK/TCK/MBTO	
4COR	3159-3168		1965	MBSO/TSK/TCK/MBSO	Rebuilt from RES power cars and PUL/PAN trailers
6COR	3041-3050		1965-66	MBSO/TSK/TSK/TFK/TSK/MBSO	Reformed of PUL/PAN coaches
4BUF	3073-3085		1938	MBTO/TCK/TRB/MBTO	
4GRI	3086-3088		1964	MBSO/TFK/TRG/MBSO	Rebuilt from 4RES units
2HAL	2601-2692		1939	MBT/DTCL	
2HAL	2693-2699		1948	MBT/DTCL	Modified 2601 series
2HAL	2700		1955	MBTO/DTCL	
4SUB	4101		1941	MBT/TT/TC/MBT	Prototype unit
4SUB	4102-4110		1944-1945	MBT/TT/TT/MBT	Production of 4101 type
4SUB	4111-4120		1946	MBT/TT/TT/MBT	Development of 4102 fleet
4SUB	4121-4130		1946-1947	MBT/TT/TT/MBT	
4SUB	4131-4171		1942-1948	MBT/TT/TT/MBT	Former 3SUB augmented with LSWR trailer
4SUB	4131-4132	‡	1969	MBS/TS/TS/MBS	Reform with 2HAL motor cars and SUB trailers
4SUB	4172-4194		1947-1948	MBT/TT/TT/MBT	1658 series 3SUB augmented with all steel trailer
4SUB	4195-4234		1942-1948	MBT/TT/TT/MBT	Former 3SUB augmented with LSWR trailer
4SUB	4235-4249		1947-1949	MBT/TT/TT/MBT	1658 series 3SUB augmented with all steel trailer
4SUB	4250-4257		1942-1948	MBT/TT/TT/MBT	Reform of 3SUB cars following collisions
4SUB	4277-4299		1948-1949	MBT/TT/TT/MBT	Final development of 4102 production fleet
4SUB	4300-4325		1945	MBT/TT/TT/MBT	Former 3SUBs augmented with all steel trailer
4SUB	4326-4354		1945-1946	MBT/TT/TT/MBT	Former 3SUBs augmented with all steel trailer
4SUB	4355		1947	MBT/TT/TT/MBT	Development of 4102 production fleet
4SUB	4377		1947	MBT/TTO/TT/MBT	Modified 4102 series design
4SUB	4378-4387		1948	MBTO/TTO/TT/MBTO	Development of 4111 series design
4SUB	4401-4431		1947	MBT/TT/TT/MBT	Former 3SUBs augmented with all steel trailer
4SUB	4432-4516		1946-1947	MBT/TT/TT/MBT	Former 3SUBs augmented with all steel trailer
4SUB	4517-4594		1947	MBT/TT/TT/MBT	Former 3SUBs augmented with all steel trailer
4SUB	4601-4608/10/3/4		1947	MBT/TT/TT/MBT	Former 3SUBs augmented with all steel trailer
4SUB	4601-4607	‡	1950	MBT/TT/TT/MBT	Development of 4111 series
4SUB	4621-4754		1949-1951	MBTO/TTO/TT/MBTO	Final 4SUB development
4DD	4001-4002	4901-4902	1949	MBT/TT/TT/MBT	Experimental double-deck units
6TC	601		1965	TBSL/TS/TC/TS/TS/TBSL	Former COR/PUL/PAN cars
7TC	900	701	1963	TBSL/TS/TS/TC/TS/TS/TCL	2BIL 2009 + 5 emu trailers
2PAN	061-066		1971	MLV/DTLV	Former 2HALs converted for parcels use

* Car numbers — no unit numbers allocated

† No unit numbers carried

‡ Number series used twice

Departmental units

184
Many emu sets have over the years been handed over to departmental or service use after revenue earning service had ceased. Converted from 3SUB motor coaches during 1959/60 a fleet of 10 two-coach de-icing units were formed, to traverse most exposed suburban routes and lay de-icing fluid when bad weather was forecast. Each vehicle of the pair was fitted with this equipment and the inner bogie of each motor coach laid the fluid. Set No 93 later renumbered 012 stands at Pulborough on 4 March 1967. *John Scrace*

185
These former 3SUB de-icing units remained in service until the early 1980s when a conversion scheme for modern de-icing/rail cleaning units was planned. Here looking rather forelorn dumped at Selhurst awaiting its move to the breaker's yard on 14 August 1979, is unit 011 taken out of service following the 1978/9 winter season. *Colin J. Marsden*

186
Old Meets New: Wimbledon Park original de-icing unit No 013 stands coupled to the 1979 converted set in the depot yard on 3 December 1979. These original ex-3SUB de-icing units were fully compatible for multiple operation with all pre-1950 built suburban stock. *Colin J. Marsden*

187
Following the withdrawal of several 4SUB units during the late 1970s it was decided to use their motor coaches for new de-icing trains. Selhurst Depot workshop was selected to undertake conversion work, which involved the complete rebuilding of each vehicle from the roof downwards. Former 4SUB No 4125 undergoes conversion work during the summer of 1979, when completed this unit became departmental unit No 009. *Colin J. Marsden*

188
To facilitate the movement of depot stores around the
Southern Region's multitude of depots, the region operate a
fleet of three departmental stores units, two of which Nos
022/3 were introduced in 1970 by converting withdrawn
2HAL motor coaches. The third unit No 024 was rebuilt from
4SUB driving vehicles during 1973. Set No 024 stands at
Hither Green in this view in a purpose built road fitted with
third rail pick up shoe protection boards. It will be noted that
this set has additional high level air and control hoses
enabling it to operate more fully with 1956/7 and 1963 built
emu stock. It is likely that the two former HAL units will be
withdrawn during 1983.   *Colin J. Marsden*